Bryan Tully

Create Your Escape

A Practical Guide for
Planning Long-Term Travel

MIKE SHUBBUCK
and TARA SHUBBUCK

First edition

ISBN: 978-0-692-54024-4

This book is for those who call the road their home
and those who opened their home to us
while we were on the road.

In memory of Zac Shlimowitz,
who still guides Tara toward her goals,
and always will.

Contents

<u>Icons to Know</u>

 General Information

 Important Tips

 He Said

 She Said

Introduction

Our Story

WHAT A DIFFERENCE two years can make. That was the length of time we went from being a pair of ambitious young professionals to becoming consumed by the thought that we had to do something big – right now. You might say we were hit by a quarter-life crisis. Looking back, it all started over the Great Barrier Reef.

Back in 2009, we were living together in Washington, D.C. After accruing nearly three weeks of vacation time at work (a yearlong process for many Americans), we decided to take our first trip to Australia. Since we both had full-time jobs, we were happy to splurge during our time off. This included tickets to the Sydney Opera House, wine tasting in the Barossa Valley, a multi-day tour around Kangaroo Island, and a three-day, two-night snorkeling trip over the Great Barrier Reef. It was an expensive vacation, but since we were only taking one big trip a year – and didn't have sizable expenses like children, a mortgage, and car payments – it seemed justified and worthwhile.

In Cairns, Australia, the boat we joined for our Great Barrier Reef trip was mostly full of SCUBA divers. Neither of us were certified divers, but we were happy to snorkel above the reefs and observe the beauty just below the water's surface. The schedule during those three days went something like this: snorkel, eat, snorkel, eat, snorkel, eat, chat and relax, then sleep. Wake up around sunrise and repeat.

During our downtime on the boat, we talked to the other passengers and found that a majority of them were friends – and experienced divers – from a diving club in Melbourne. However, there was a younger diver, John, from Cheddar, England, who wasn't part of the Melbourne group and was still learning. John, 19, was in Australia by himself and had begun his SCUBA certification in Malaysia before arriving. He had recently finished high school and was visiting Australia as part of an around-the-world gap year before entering university.

Since this was our first time meeting someone traveling on a gap year, we were inquisitive, though we found ourselves asking superficial questions – like what country he enjoyed most. Even though we both had backpacked around Europe, we were unable to connect with John on other levels because we couldn't understand his motivation for wanting to go on such a long trip. In many cultures, it's common to take a gap year while young, but it's not something most Americans do.

While we enjoyed listening to John's stories, we kept a "we'll never do that" type of attitude. It was mostly because of where we were in life. At that point, we had already finished our undergraduate degrees and joined the workforce. Our jobs were challenging and secure during a time when others were having trouble finding employment because of the recession. Additionally, we enjoyed being social young professionals in a cosmopolitan city. We felt as though everything in our lives was going well, and we couldn't even imagine leaving it all to travel long-term.

After our vacation in Australia, the next few years were nice, but highly predictable. We talked about marriage and were working hard toward promotions and saving money to buy a condo and the pug we always wanted – our version of the American dream and the path that society teaches. But much like the film Inception, John from Cheddar, England, had planted an idea that reappeared unexpectedly.

It was the beginning of 2011 when we first started talking about our next big steps in life. Marriage? Yes. Children? No. Buy our first home in D.C.? Maybe. We didn't know if we were ready to settle down, so we started thinking about our future and what we really wanted. We enjoyed our jobs, but the same complaints came up weekly, even daily. They weren't as fulfilling as they used to be.

For months, we had a difficult time determining our potential next steps with our careers, housing, and which city we would settle in. We began questioning a lot about our path, and before we knew it, we were in quarter-life crisis mode, wondering what we actually wanted.

We finally realized we were at a crossroads. We had no anchors – like a car, property, pets, or children – and we both were comfortable with leaving our jobs at the same time. As we considered the statement, "There will never be a perfect time to do x, y, and z – you just have to do it," we realized it was actually our perfect time. This was our opportunity to make any number of life-altering moves: start our own company, move to a new city, or take an adult-style gap year, essentially a career break. "Let's just quit our jobs and travel around the world" was something we occasionally said in jest, probably thanks to John planting that idea. But at the heart of every joke is a kernel of truth, and we began to question the underlying honesty of this little joke by asking, "Why can't we?"

The only thing stopping us from veering "off course" was our own inaction. While traveling the world is an exciting idea, we weren't immediately comfortable with it. It would be a bold and adventurous move, but leaving for more than a year would shake up our lives. Way too many "what if" scenarios popped up that made us question its practicality. You know the type: What if we run out of money along the way? What if we can't find jobs when we return? And what if we aren't as good travel partners as we thought? Being unemployed, out of money, and stuck in a foreign country with someone you don't want to travel with is a worst-case scenario that would give anyone pause when planning a trip of this magnitude. But we knew the possibility of that happening was so improbable that it was irrational to be paralyzed by those fears.

After a month of talking, we shifted to taking action. When it came to determining the "right" decision, the idea of doing something big won out. We decided that if we were going to break the rules, we were going to break them completely. And what's more fun than doing what you want for a year? So we got married, quit our jobs, and went on a 14-month honeymoon of a lifetime, stepping into 26 countries on three continents. We front-loaded our marriage with a lifetime of memories, and it was a joyride we will never forget.

Why we wrote this book

If you picked up this book, you are independent and adventurous. We know that type because we are that type. But even the best coordinators and most savvy travelers seek tips, ideas, and on-the-ground information. When we were planning our big trip, we searched for a comprehensive guide to around-the-world travel for couples, but came up empty-handed. We relied on blogs and other Internet resources, clogging each other's inboxes with links to articles. Planning would have been much easier if the majority of information we needed was in a book that we could have read, highlighted, and discussed.

Sometimes you also want to know that you aren't crazy, even when your friends and family suspect you may be. Before our trip, no one in our social circles had even thought to take a 'round-the-world trip (also referred to as an RTW), let alone do it. Even though the idea of being trailblazers is fun, we needed to build our confidence a little. After all, we were about to quit our jobs and leave a secure life to travel. We definitely felt crazy. We knew there were like-minded people out there, people who had already accomplished what we dreamed of doing, and we wanted to hear their story.

This is the book we wish we had access to from the beginning of the planning process to help guide us. Even though you can glean valuable information from guidebooks, it is encouraging to read another couple's full account of the planning process, how they divvied up responsibilities, and what they found to be most important in hindsight.

How this book will help you

Our expertise is couples' travel, but the information in this book is for any potential long-term traveler and designed to serve as a comprehensive pre-departure planning tool. Preparation is crucial, and we want you to know what to expect. Our planning period lasted nearly the same length of time as our entire RTW journey. While you could buy a ticket out of the country and leave tomorrow, you will surely encounter difficulties along the way that you could have prevented with a little research and action. For example, why lose money paying exorbitant ATM fees when you could have them all reimbursed at the end of each month? This book will ensure you don't forget anything, so you can be 100% proactive and avoid the sticky situations that cause you to be reactive.

Those traveling with a friend or significant other will glean valuable information – like how to share responsibilities and work well together – from the suggestions and personal experiences we each share throughout the chapters. If you are a solo traveler, reading two points of view will give you a better understanding of each task and aid in decision-making. Even if you are traveling with children, you can use the book as a base while also brainstorming fun ways to get your kids involved. For example, during the pre-departure period, they can present book reports on the countries they are most looking forward to visiting. These can include important tidbits like currency information, national language, and which ingredients are used in the local cuisine that might be allergens to someone in the family.

Some chapters in this book will also be useful to those who are not backpacking for months on end or planning an RTW trip. We provide tips for juggling practicality, fashion, and comfort when packing for a trip. If you have never bought medical travel insurance before, we'll help you determine whether you need it and how to choose the right one if you do. And our tips for saving money and reducing your possessions are applicable to anyone, even those who do not plan to travel any time soon.

Who can travel long-term?

Four words: have passport, will travel.

Anyone with gusto can take the necessary steps to turn their dream into a reality. You don't have to be a member of the "one percent" or have a location-independent job. While on the road, we met all types of long-term travelers with different financial situations. Many people, like us, were using their life savings. Some were traveling slowly and freelancing or picking up odd jobs along their route. Others volunteered in exchange for free room and board. And many people were living a nomadic life through a combination of these things. They all did whatever they could to prolong a satisfying and transformative adventure. Some of these people had never even traveled internationally before!

Additionally, it's not true that backpackers have to be young and single. We met couples, groups, and solo travelers from every age group, and some were even traveling with children. How cool would it be to give your child a real international education? It's certainly an experience they will never forget.

If you are passionate about having a long-term adventure, start saving for it now and just make it happen. Don't sit around waiting for your "perfect time to travel," because it isn't always easy to recognize that you've hit that point in your life. Once you start the preparation work, you will feel your journey beginning, and it will become something you won't want to give up.

Without a doubt, our round-the-world trip was the once-in-a-lifetime experience everyone said it would be. Followers of our journey lived vicariously through us, saying, "I wish I could do that!" And we responded, "You can!" Fear, lack of funds, too many commitments, or a combination might be holding them – and you – back. Or perhaps you are ready and do not need further convincing. As you read on, you'll see that preparing for and taking an RTW trip is not just for the wealthy or retired. If you stay committed to the goal, it is something anyone can achieve.

CHAPTER

Create a Pre-Departure Planning Schedule 12+ Months Prior to Departure

WE SAT INSIDE the N1 gas station in Egilsstadir, Iceland, eagerly awaiting the first exotic meal of our 14-month trip around the world trip: reindeer burgers. Our guesthouse's friendly caretaker, Gudsteinn, highly recommended both the restaurant and meal as local favorites. Back home in the United States, restaurants inside gas stations aren't known for their culinary achievements, but Iceland continually surprised us.

For one thing, summer in this island country didn't mean an escape from near-freezing temperatures. However, the weather gave us the opportunity to see puffins, reindeer, and a glacial lake. Roads that were normally closed during the winter had just reopened, allowing us to drive on Ring Road around the whole island. Otherwise, we most likely wouldn't have been able to visit Egilsstadir and eat a reindeer burger for the first time in our lives.

The burgers were simple – a bun, patty, and blue cheese topping – but the ingredients were complementary and delicious. It's an experience we would've never had had it not been for Gudsteinn. Likewise, since he learned just how adventurous we were, he brought in local specialties for us to try at the guesthouse, like skyr (similar to yogurt) and hardfiskur (dried fish that you spread butter on). It was during memorable experiences like these when it hit us that this crazy idea of traveling the world was really happening.

We were only on day five of our 'round-the-world trip (also referred to as an RTW) and it was already worth writing home about. One night after exploring the nearby area, we decided to take our chances with the shaky Internet connection. The guesthouse's wireless router spat out a weak signal, probably because of the remote location of this east Iceland town. Luckily, it was strong enough to log into our email and read a message from Mike's parents, who were receiving our mail during our RTW.

Their email said that the check we wrote for our last month's rent was declined due to a freeze on our checking account. The apartment management company was fining us with a late fee plus a service charge, totaling more than $100 USD. This didn't make sense to us. We thought we had tied up all loose ends before departing the United States. Now we had to figure out a solution while on a different continent.

We decided to start with our bank and tried to call them on Skype using the wireless network. After many dropped calls, Gudsteinn graciously invited us into his office to use the Ethernet connection. Finally, we were able to connect with a customer service representative who told us what went wrong: Negligence on the part of another employee resulted in our two-month-old account being flagged as unverified even though we had taken the required steps to activate the account. Ultimately, the bank took responsibility and not only used its own money to pay the late fee and service charge, but also mailed a new rent check to the apartment management company on our behalf.

It's easy to look at the situation and say that everything turned out well and not to think twice about it. But the ease at which the situation was resolved proved that our preparation paid off. Without planning and putting a system in place to catch such issues, we would've owed costly fees and may have even damaged our credit score. This is why it's crucial to plan prior to leaving home for an extended period of time. Since we took our pre-departure preparation work seriously, we saved ourselves from having to deal with problems like this for the rest of our RTW. In fact, during our 14 months on the road, this was the only major financial hiccup we encountered.

The importance of planning

The scope of pre-departure planning extends beyond booking hotels and plane tickets. With a trip that will last for more than five consecutive months, you'll need to do what we call "wrapping up your home life." This necessary preparation begins with your personal affairs and extends to every other aspect of your life, from freezing your credit to authorizing power of attorney to sharing news of the trip with family, friends, and your employer. It's purposefully extensive and comprehensive so you can hit the road carefree. Otherwise, you risk spending hours trying to find a secure Internet connection to complete the sale of your car or set up travel notifications for credit cards.

Convincing a potential travel partner to join you

Solo travel definitely has its perks, like being the master of your itinerary and every decision associated with it (both Tara and Mike traveled through Europe for extended periods without each other), but the memories you share with a travel partner can be thrilling, and you won't be able stop talking about the time you watched the sunrise from the top of sand dunes in Namibia. This will be a special once-in-a-lifetime experience, and having someone to share it with will end up being a highlight in and of itself.

If you do have a relative, best friend, or better half who is hesitant to join you, it may take some work to persuade him or her. After all, extended travel is an obvious time commitment, not to mention the necessary sacrifices that must be made, like quitting your job, leaving your home, and being far away from friends and family. Be empathetic to all of his or her concerns, and don't forget that you did (or maybe still do!) have similar thoughts.

If your travel partner needs convincing (that is, you are the driving force behind this trip), then take a step back and think logically about the reasons why now is the perfect time in your lives to travel. Make a thorough game plan before you try to persuade your potential travel partner to drop everything to join you. Crafting a solid argument may also be just what you need to push some of your own doubts from your mind.

First, determine how you'll begin the conversation, what main points you want to discuss, all the positive reasons you have for taking the trip, and ways to address concerns or negative thoughts.

Present the information in a way that is easy for him or her to understand and show your passion while you talk about the benefits and reasons you want to pursue the trip (exotic pictures and sample itineraries will help too). Also, be prepared to address logistical and financial concerns by laying out your monthly planning goals and your plan for funding the trip. Presenting a thoroughly thought-out idea makes it easier to persuade someone to get on board. Preparation shows confidence and confidence is persuasive. Make it difficult to resist joining you!

It may take a few conversations, but the more you discuss it and stress the benefits, the more confident and comfortable you both will feel with the decision. This is a brave, bold move, and it's completely normal to feel a little scared when you're doing something that breaks the mold.

It's okay if the thought of being so detailed and organized makes you cringe. Having to plan anything but a list of places you want to visit may not sound very exciting, but it's the cornerstone of your RTW and an absolute necessity if you want to get the most out of your big adventure. An important mantra to remember is "prepare now, relax later." But this stage doesn't have to be boring or exhausting, and shouldn't be. For many people, planning and getting excited about the trip is part of the fun. So look at the process from a different perspective. If you're going to spend the next 12 months planning an exciting international trip, make it a pleasurable hobby or an opportunity to strengthen weaknesses and learn new skills, like how to budget, maintain spreadsheets, and even practice self-control. Some may be soft skills, but others will be applicable to future career opportunities and can be added to your resume. Learn from this experience and grow from it!

One of the most important things to remember as you plan for your trip is that there are no right or wrong decisions. You can pick up tips and tricks from fellow travelers, but there will never be a one-style-fits-all approach to planning, packing, or traveling. And you'll even find that your own approach will evolve as you gain more experience and travel longer with your partner. Likewise, you must determine your own preferences based on your comfort level and through trial and error. Just because a luggage salesman suggests taking a 40-liter pack does not mean you have to purchase it. Maybe it worked for him when he trekked across Africa, but it may not fit the gear and winter coat you'll need for hiking on glaciers in Alaska.

Without further ado, let's start planning for your trip!

Buy a world map and a container of pins

It'll be easy to get distracted during this process, but you never want to lose sight of your ultimate goal: You are going to travel around the world! Even more exciting is that you will share the experience with an awesome travel partner. That might be simultaneously thrilling and frightening, but let's focus on the thrill of it. After all, excitement is contagious, and it'll be great reinforcement during the preparation process and the key for staying on track.

Visualizing your trip will do wonders to keep your final goal in sight. The best way to do this is to purchase a world map and hang it on your wall. This reminder of your trip should bring a smile to your face every time you see it. Furthermore, it is a concrete way to help you consider a tentative route. Buy pins, too, so you and your partner can mark locations that each of you are interested in visiting.

Think of the map as an ideas board. You won't necessarily visit all the places you pin, but at least you will have a feel for your individual and shared interests. If you have friends living abroad, flag those countries with a pin. Do you have dream locations you want to visit? Mark them too. Where can you participate in once-in-a-lifetime activities or festivals along the way? Think big! You can always cut back on the number of places you visit, but at this stage, let your enthusiasm be your guide.

Make a checklist and assign tasks

The fastest way to start arguments with your travel partner is to divide the workload unequally. If there is too much pressure on one person before, during, or after your travels, tension will build and fights will ensue. Nobody wants to do everything, and with a trip like this, no one should. Learning to divide pre-departure responsibilities between you and your travel partner is good practice for how you will handle life on the road.

The first step is to compile the most time-consuming tasks so you can make them your top priorities. Goals like choosing a travel insurance provider may seem daunting (and can be!), but after collecting information and reading the fine print, it should not take very long to settle on one (we're talking a matter of weeks, perhaps, but not months). The things you want to consider first are those that require more time, like budgeting and saving money, and those that are not fully in your control, like whether you will be able to sell your house in a timely manner. Drawing up a list is your first step, and then you can start divvying up the tasks and nailing down a comprehensive schedule for completion.

 Creating your first to-do list

You're ready to make a year-out checklist to stay organized, but what do you start with? Here are a few important time-consuming tasks that you will want to focus on at least one year prior to departure. We'll talk in-depth about how to reach these goals throughout the next couple chapters, but you can start brainstorming ideas now.

• **Money**: Money matters are king. If you don't have a discretionary fund, you'll have to work toward a savings goal. Calculate what that goal should be by using the formula we provide in The Cost of Travel and How to Make a Budget chapter, and then brainstorm ways to decrease spending and increase monthly savings, income, or both.

- **Property**: Whether you rent or own, you will need to decide if you need to break a lease, find a tenant, or sell your place.

- **Possessions**: Sell, donate, trash, or store your stuff? What will you do with your vehicle?

- **Pets**: Your pug can't come with you. Traveling with animals will severely limit the locations you can visit and the activities you'll be able to participate in. You can make your trip a pet-friendly one, but you'll need to figure out how to make that happen. If you decide to leave your pets at home, ask family members or trusted friends to watch them until you return.

- **People**: Do you have children or adults you're responsible for? Unless they will be traveling with you, set up a plan to care for them in your absence.

Once you make a firm decision for how you will handle everything, determine what steps you'll need to take to execute each plan. Will you work on these tasks solo or will you and your travel partner help each other?

As you brainstorm time-consuming tasks, begin to assemble them into a checklist so you can determine your next steps. Your list may include finding a part-time job, canceling memberships and subscriptions so you can save more money, and repairing things around the house that will help attract potential renters or buyers. Then, assign each action item based on your and your travel partner's interests and personal strengths.

As visual people, we found it helpful to list everything on paper with one of our names and an attainable deadline next to each assignment. Every time we completed a task, we made a big show out of crossing it off with a marker. It felt good to see our progress and know we were one step closer to making our trip a reality.

Post your paper list in an easily seen location to get the most from it. Our checklist stayed on our daily gathering spot: the dining room table. There was no way for us to miss or ignore it. We each set our own digital reminders as well, but had we saved the checklist in digital form only, we might not have opened it on a regular basis. A hard copy at home provided an easy way to keep track of our own responsibilities while seeing if the other person was staying on pace as well. Another idea is to hang a whiteboard, chalkboard, or large poster paper in a prominent spot. Customize it by color-coding each other's tasks so it's easier to identify what's left on your to-do list.

Start attacking your long-term goals as early in the process as possible, and mix in a few easier and shorter tasks as well. By making quick progress on simple tasks, you'll boost your confidence while having the opportunity to take a break from a larger project.

There will undoubtedly be responsibilities that neither of you are particularly interested in attacking, so take advantage of having a travel partner by rotating assignments. Whoever accepts the first undesirable task can skip the next one. Learning to alternate roles will also come in handy once you start traveling. While you both will likely have your own on-the-road roles, you'll want to switch off every now and then to avoid burnout.

The key is to keep a balance in the workload. There may also come a time when you have to pick up the slack because your travel partner isn't feeling up to snuff. You'll want to be able to rely on each other, so use the planning process as an opportunity to better understand and anticipate your travel partner's strengths and weakness, as well as your own.

As you come across tasks that you normally wouldn't want to handle, step up and accept the challenge of turning a weakness into a new skill. For example, if you're an introvert and the task involves calling various companies to receive quotes, seize the opportunity. Interacting with strangers may be intimidating at first, but it is a huge part of a traveler's life. Even if you are an extrovert, this will be an easy way to practice becoming a better communicator before you encounter people with whom you do not share a common language. Being the go-to person to ask locals for directions, departure times, and a host of other things can wear down anyone, but if you are able to switch every now and then, it should prevent both of you from burning out.

The size of your checklist will ebb and flow as you complete prep work, and new goals organically arise. Assign attainable deadlines and stay on top of them, but remember to prioritize (headings like "Nine Months Out" and "Three Months Out" are helpful) so you can focus first on activities that will take the longest or need to be completed before others can begin. You can either rewrite and revise your list on a consistent basis to keep it neat and remove completed tasks, or you may want to just continue adding to the same list to keep track of everything you've done.

Create realistic deadlines

The biggest difference between a to-do list and a goal-oriented checklist is that to-do lists are typically just lists (such as pharmacy, post office, grocery store) without hard deadlines for each item.

The importance of a completion date is that it will propel you to action. Without deadlines, to-do lists have a tendency to spiral out of control to the point where they become too long and unmanageable. But what you're making is not your typical to-do list; you are wrapping up your "at-home life" so you can travel carefree for months on end.

Creating attainable deadlines can be one of the most difficult parts of putting together an RTW checklist. Here are three steps to remember when determining a hard date:

1. Visualize every step and be realistic. With your ultimate goal in mind, think about everything you'll have to do to reach it. How long will x, y, and z take if you give them your undivided attention?

2. Give yourself extra time. Obstacles are bound to crop up, whether they are unforeseen sub-tasks or actual roadblocks. Give yourself sufficient time to work through these things, and rejoice if you finish early without any problems.

3. Work step by step and evaluate your deadline as you make progress. If things are looking good and you finish before deadline, celebrate! But if each step is taking longer than expected, consider pushing back the deadline you created. There's no harm in it unless it's causing a negative ripple effect. As you work through each task and continue to set deadlines, you'll get a feel for how you work and whether your deadline predictions are accurate and attainable.

Setting specific deadlines is essential for an RTW checklist, since a completion date will force you to finish assignments. Remember, it is never too early to start planning and knocking goals off your checklist. A year may seem incredibly far away, but it will fly by, so we encourage you to set deadlines that aren't too long and will keep you moving forward at a steady pace. Likewise, stay focused and have heart. If you find you are unable to meet deadlines, you may be tempted to ignore them completely – but don't! Just adjust them accordingly. Our RTW checklist swelled to have dozens of items. Can you imagine how stressed we would have been if we let deadlines slide by and allowed our tasks to pile up?

 ### Like a wedding, save the date

Setting a leave date is probably one of the most difficult decisions you will have to make during your planning. You can talk from dawn to dusk about the "big trip" you are planning, but unless you commit to a date, it lacks teeth. Looking back, we planned our wedding and trip at the same time – and by ourselves! Doing this required strict planning and irrevocable deadlines.

How do you set a leave date? First, look at your finances and any serious commitments you have to fulfill. Then, determine when you realistically can leave without any remaining concerns. Once you set that date, be as committed to it as a wedding date. Circle it on all your calendars. Mark it in your brain. Buy your first one-way plane ticket or book your first hotel. Make it real. Deadlines with consequences will help you to hit them. The benefit from setting a leave date also extends to creating a comprehensive timeline for your RTW checklist. Now that you know when you will leave, you can work backward to set deadlines.

Of course, a couple things slipped through the cracks. For example, we waited too long to sell our bed and were forced to give it away. Mike wanted to wait to sell it because he felt we'd have ample opportunity to sleep on uncomfortable surfaces during the trip (he was right). Whereas Tara was nervous it would not sell at the last minute (she was right) and preferred to advertise it a couple weeks before leaving. We waited until the last minute to list it, and it never sold. Considering we attached a mental price tag to it, we lost out on easy money.

Let's look at an example of a long-term goal that requires many sub-tasks so you have a better understanding of what to consider when setting deadlines. If you own a vehicle, you already know it is a large financial responsibility that you will need to sort out before leaving. Will you sell the vehicle? Will you store it, and who will maintain or look after it? Don't forget that vehicles require insurance even if they are not being driven. This difficult decision will need to be made first before you can develop deadlines for such a task. Your friends and family will often prove to be a savior in situations like this; they may offer to buy your vehicle or propose a flexible way out for you. But we don't recommend waiting in hopes that a friend or family member will bail you out. Instead, let's assume you will proactively move forward with selling your car.

As with everything, there are myriad factors that could change every aspect. For the sake of making this example easier to explain, we will assume you own the car outright (things become more complicated if you if still owe payments on the vehicle).
If you do opt to sell your vehicle, determine when you can start living without it. As with everything in the planning process, use your leave date as a guide for working backward to create deadlines. You most likely rely on your vehicle to get around, so selling it too soon may cripple your ability to go easily from place to place. Likewise, if you wait too long to sell it, you may be stuck with it or feel forced to accept a far lower sale price than you want.

Let's say you think you can live your final month at home without a vehicle. This final sell-by date is the deadline you must work against. If your strategy is unsuccessful and you are unable to meet that deadline, you'll need to create a worst-case scenario plan to execute during your last month at home (more later on what that plan might entail).

Now that you know your final deadline, start with the basics. Begin with a little research to gauge the demand of the make and model you own. The Kelley Blue Book estimated value is a good place to start when it comes to understanding what your vehicle is worth. You can find a printed copy at your local library or use the company's website to punch in your vehicle's specs and determine its value based on your location. Obviously, the more money you can get for your vehicle, the more time you should invest in making sure you achieve a fair price. Since this is a large and time-consuming task, we recommend identifying smaller sub-tasks, with your end goal still being to sell the car a month before you leave.

Your vehicle's value is hinged on how well you take care of it. Before listing it, look into the cost of touch-ups and improvements that may transform a car from fair to good condition. If you bring it in for repairs, be sure to keep the receipt so you can prove to potential buyers that parts are new and the vehicle is in top shape. Keep in mind that if you have a clunker of a car that you won't make much money off of, then scrap this task for something more pressing – you can always dump your wreck for scrap metal if it comes down to it.

Once the time comes to sell, we recommend that you immediately list the car everywhere. Everywhere may seem like a broad term, but you want to give your car as many chances for sale as possible. And the longer the vehicle is on the market, the more time you have to generate interest. If a potential buyer does contact you sooner than you hoped, you may be able to agree to delay the final sale until your departure date is closer. This is a more favorable scenario than having to desperately execute your backup plan.

When you privately sell your car to an individual, you must prepare a bill of sale that documents the transaction terms and serves as a legal receipt. You can find more information about the bill of sale and how to transfer the title at your local Department of Motor Vehicles.

If you haven't been contacted with genuine interest and you fear that time is running out, you may want to sell directly to a dealership or used-car retailer, though you will most likely net much less than you would receive in a private sale. Another option is to look into dealer consignment. Dealerships often sell cars on consignment, paying you after the car sells but keeping a percentage.

You can see from this example that some tasks aren't as simple as performing a little research, reviewing information, and making a decision. You have to consider the bigger picture when figuring out what else needs to be completed and in what order. The important thing is to start thinking ahead – think about which sub-tasks will be the most time-consuming and start those first. If everything is moving more quickly than you anticipated, move up your other deadlines. If you are working more slowly than you thought you would, ask yourself why that is happening. Perhaps you are finding it difficult to make time for this project and need to restructure your schedule to maximize your free time. Or maybe there is more work than you expected and you therefore have to push back deadlines.

 Stay ahead of the devil & make a detailed checklist

Review the sample checklist on the following pages to gain a better understanding of how to create sub-tasks from a goal (this one applies to selling your vehicle) and set deadlines with the bigger picture in mind.

10-12 months out

1. Settle on a latest-possible sale date that works for you.
- Can you rely on public transport to get around after you sell?
- Can you carpool or borrow a friend or family member's car as a stopgap if your vehicle sells early?

2. Determine and begin any repairs or improvements that are necessary to make a sale.
- Simple inexpensive fixes, like having the oil changed, also show potential buyers that you maintain your vehicle.
- Detail your vehicle before a showing.

3. Research your vehicle's value after repairs and touchups are made.
- Look at the Kelley Blue Book.
- Search online and in the newspaper for your make and model to see what other vehicles are selling for.
- Determine a minimum price you want to sell at but start listing at the highest possible price.

4. Research options for advertising the sale of your vehicle.
- Classified websites.
- In-print and online publications.
- Parking your vehicle along a busy road with a for sale sign and phone number.

9 months out

1. Advertise your vehicle.
- Write a detailed description and take pictures.
- Respond immediately to interested parties.

2. Research what to do in the event of a private sale.
- Understand what legal requirements exist, like drawing up the bill of sale and transferring the title to the new owner.
- Find out where your best local resource for information is

(maybe the clerk's office or Department of Motor Vehicles).

5-8 months out

1. Continue advertising your vehicle as listings expire or new opportunities arise.

2. Make a list of dealerships that buy used vehicles.

3. Make a list of dealerships that sell on consignment.

4. Gather information from the dealerships that sell on consignment.
- What is the process?
- What is the average time it takes a car to sell? (If they recommend 2 or more months, then move the sub-task below from 2 months out to 3 to 4 months out.)
- Are there guarantees?
- Would they consider purchasing the car if it doesn't sell in time?

3-4 months out

1. Reduce your vehicle's advertised price.

2. Gather bids from your list of dealerships that buy used vehicles.

2 months out

1. Further reduce the advertised price to the lowest amount you are willing to sell at.

2. Bring your car to a dealership that sells on consignment.

1 month out

1. Initiate worst-case scenario plan. This might be:
- Sell to a dealership
- Donate to a nonprofit organization for a charitable tax deduction
- Give your car to your cousin who just graduated
- Other

Ultimately, the best way to decide on a deadline is to imagine yourself working on the task for hours without distractions. Realistically think about how many consecutive days it would take to complete while juggling other deadlines and day-to-day things that are unrelated to your trip. Add in extra time to account for obstacles or unexpected problems. Give each task the attention it deserves and adjust the deadline if you need to before moving on.

Set aside time to plan your trip and keep your eye on the prize

Now that goals and deadlines are spinning through your head, do you know how you'll find sufficient time to complete everything on your checklist? We'll just come out and say it: Scheduling time to work on your pre-departure planning will be difficult for you and your travel partner if you both have demanding full-time jobs. But don't stress! Slow progress is better than no progress. This is the reason we encourage you to start planning so early.

In the beginning, you might be eager to tackle your to-do list every night after getting home from work. But beware of fatigue. It is best to start by devoting a couple weeknights and weekend days to "RTW Planning Time," then expand as needed. During this time, cancel out all distractions and focus on your tasks. We found that alternating nights between high-stress planning (things like budgeting or insurance research) and simple activities (like sorting possessions into sell and donate piles or discussing festivals we want to attend on our RTW) kept us from feeling burned out. Additionally, creating RTW-only workspaces – like a desk at the library or a corner in your home – will help you to focus better on tasks and separate your trip from your "everyday" life. Creating a space where you and your travel partner can concentrate also includes cutting digital distractions, like switching your phone to airplane mode, turning off your Internet router, or deactivating your social media accounts. Ignore them now, and later you can tweet a picture from a mountaintop in the Himalayas.

 Carrots are good, but beer is better

A couple months passed between the time Tara and I first talked about the trip and when we began setting the goals that would help make it a reality. At first, the magnitude of the trip – all the planning and how it would ultimately change our lives – made me feel paralyzed. Part of me even thought we were starting the planning process too early.

Tara was exactly the opposite. She was kinetic, knowing we wouldn't be able to wrap up our lives in a matter of months. "We need to start now!" The key, she told me, was to take baby steps. After setting and meeting a few easily attainable deadlines, I realized that only a few months of planning wouldn't cut it. There was a lot to do, but I lacked good time management and had to figure out how to maximize my free time so we could complete all the necessary planning for the trip. As the scales slowly tipped from pet project to life transformation, I started to believe more and more in our ability to pull off the trip.

During this time, we also began reining in our expenses by reducing unnecessary spending. Two of the first things we cut back on were social drinking and going out (to restaurants and bars). Minimizing social activities had a dual purpose of helping us save faster while also staying more focused on planning the trip. Instead of filling weekends and nights with parties, concerts, and sports games, we tried to juggle deadlines and goals without completely neglecting our friends.

Since we cut back on drinking, Tara was able to leverage the occasional beer as a metaphorical carrot to get me to complete arduous tasks that I was putting off. Knowing that a tasty pilsner would be waiting for me at the end of the task was motivation enough for me to get moving. While the trip itself should have been obvious motivation, it was sometimes difficult to see it as such since it was still so far away (a whole year!). Something as small as a beer motivated me, and finding that carrot for your travel partner will help you both work on your checklist, especially when it seems like you're so far away from leaving.

Hitting that "unsocial" button on your life may seem difficult at first, so make sure your friends understand and support your RTW Planning Time. Social activities might be tempting, but limit them to the nights you're taking off from planning your trip. If you are keeping your RTW a secret from everyone until you're farther along in your planning, you can politely decline invitations, tell others that you're trying to save money by limiting nights out, or tell them that those nights are "me time" for a personal project you're working on.

CHAPTER IN REVIEW

❑ Hang a world map in your home to remind you of your ultimate goal. Start planning a route by marking the locations you want to visit.

❑ Create a checklist of important long-term tasks and assign responsibilities to yourself and your travel partner.

❑ Find creative ways to keep each other motivated to stay focused on completing the tasks on your checklist.

❑ Set reasonable deadlines by working backward and thinking about the sub-tasks that might be involved. Once everything is written out, section them off into monthly goals, and then set specific dated deadlines for each task. Adjust all deadlines accordingly if you find you need more time.

❑ Balance your social life with planning for your RTW by setting aside time for each.

CHAPTER 2

Reduce Your Possessions
12 Months Prior to Departure

YOU ARE ABOUT to embark on a journey that requires living a minimalistic lifestyle. A long-term traveler carries his or her life in one main bag, where there is little or no room for excess. You won't find superfluous hoodies or pairs of "just in case" shoes adding extra weight to a backpacker's bag. Sometimes even souvenirs from a recently visited city are skipped in lieu of maximizing space or to keep the pack at a manageable weight.

When we were traveling, we were constantly evaluating our things. Do we need so many socks? Shorts? Nice shirts? Our goal was to keep only what we would use on a daily or weekly basis.

Don't wait until you leave home to switch into traveler mode, though. Instead, ease yourself into it now by practicing a minimalistic lifestyle before you hit the road. Then, by the time you're ready to leave for your trip, you'll have learned to value utility and shun frivolousness.

Being able to pare down your possessions to only what you need and will actually use won't be a shift that happens overnight. You have to first be able to identify things that are excessive and also feel comfortable with offloading them.

Change the way you view material objects

Most people don't use a majority of their practical, non-decorative items on a weekly or even monthly basis. Maybe you save much of it because you think you'll use it one day, or perhaps some things were gifts that you feel obligated to keep. Accumulating items like these might bring you toward hoarder territory, but your trip is going to help pull you out. If you were looking for the perfect excuse and opportunity to unclutter your home, you now have one: you must minimize your possessions before your RTW.

If you haven't considered paring down or were hoping to store everything you own, think about the bigger picture. You are probably taking this trip because you're attuned to what you want out of life. Once-in-a-lifetime experiences, not necessarily material possessions, are the things that add meaning to your life and will make you most happy. Take this same frame of mind and apply it to the things you own. Even if the thought of such an undertaking seems overwhelming or you aren't interested in the sell-all-my-worldly-possessions approach, there are practical benefits to paring down as much as possible.

 Need that extra motivation?

Here are some benefits to shrinking your worldly possessions:

1. This is a great opportunity to offload things you've been meaning to get rid of.

2. Selling your possessions will add cash in your World Travel Fund.

3. You will have less to maintain, manage, and worry about from afar.

4. Packing before you leave will be easier when you have less to box and store. (Bonus: Being able to fit your possessions in a friend or family member's attic carries no cost!)

5. There will be less to move and sort upon your return, making you more mobile.

6. You will emerge from this stage of your life with only the possessions you really need and want.

Admittedly, even when presented with these benefits, it took us a while to realize we should drastically reduce our possessions. We initially hoped to save nearly everything because that seemed like the natural thing to do. Never before did we have a pressing reason to get rid of more than just a few things. When you move to a new home, you don't necessarily spend months deciding what you will keep. It's easier to save nearly everything. But after researching the cost of renting a storage unit, we began to rethink our plan. We didn't like the thought of monthly fees cutting into our World Travel Fund. It made us wonder if the value of the items we'd keep would justify renting a unit. Sure, our possessions held a sentimental value, but did it make logical sense to save everything?

Now we had the opportunity to look at what we were doing from a larger perspective. We asked, "What does this trip mean to us?" We were quitting our jobs, terminating our apartment lease, and redirecting the path of our lives to do what? Travel? There was so much more to it than that, though. Our outlook on life had changed, and we realized that what we wanted to keep in our lives had changed, too. The essence of our RTW was mobility, freedom, and letting go. Throwing everything into an expensive storage unit would have been the antithesis of what we were striving to achieve. We wanted to free ourselves of any anchors that kept us in one spot. We wouldn't be able to explore fully new options later on if we were tied to stacks of boxes back home. Instead of viewing it as a loss, we thought of it as a physical and mental cleanse and spent months clearing the space around us.

 Pre-minimizing may not be a real phrase, but you can do it

Tara's family is big on exchanging gifts during the holidays. We didn't want to accumulate additional possessions while paring down, so she talked to them about our situation to make sure we were all on the same page.

If your family also exchanges presents during the holidays, it's important that you approach the subject delicately. Explain that while you appreciate their generosity, you can only store and carry so many items. If they insist on exchanging gifts, ask them to consider giving a practical gift card or making a donation to your World Travel Fund. Great gift card options can include pharmacies, grocery stores, outdoor recreational stores, and prepaid debit cards.

While we were firmly fixed with downsizing as much as possible, the reality was that we still had things we wanted to keep. In a fortuitous turn of events, Tara's aunt and uncle offered to store our remaining possessions in their attic. Once their offer was on the table, we had to resist the temptation to save more than we needed just because we had a free and sizable place to store our things. This was an opportunity to be seized, not squandered. Throughout the process, we kept asking ourselves, "Why continue to store, pack, and move items that we barely used?" Ultimately, we were able to fit everything we owned inside an SUV (when stacked, both of our possessions were less than 5' x 5' x 5'). And upon our return, we were thankful there weren't a ton of boxes to sort through. It was a refreshing opportunity to build a new life around the new people we felt we had become.

Determine what doesn't add value

Ultimately, what you do with your possessions is entirely up to you. Uncluttering is not a mandatory step in the planning process, but we strongly encourage it for the reasons we listed earlier. Even if you don't want to pare down that much, our strategies will help you recognize what is taking up space but not adding value to your daily life, which will be useful once you hit the road.

If living a more minimal lifestyle is something you want to pursue, start as soon as possible even if you aren't able to devote much time at first. Follow the exercises and strategies we recommend in this chapter. Our plan of attack helped us get rid of nearly everything we owned and will also put you on your way to fitting all your worldly possessions in only a few boxes.

First, let "What doesn't add value but takes up space?" be your mantra.

This seemingly simple question might be difficult to answer, and not just because your home is full of the things you own and love, but because you probably don't realize how much you actually own. Many things sit out of sight, hidden in cabinets, the back of your closet, or in containers you haven't sorted through for years.

To understand how and where to begin, just start simply.

Walk through your front door and make your way through each room. Look at everything you own, opening every single drawer, cupboard, and closet door. As you do this, take the time to really think about your possessions. Count how much glassware you have. Try to remember the last time you wore every pair of shoes you own. Sift through your junk drawer and think about why you've never emptied it. How about the candles that have never been lit, your collection of hotel toiletries, and the margarita mix you still haven't opened? Start to question the things you have that are collecting dust.

This exercise should give you a more thorough understanding of the amount of things you own. Now that you have begun visualizing your possessions, you have to determine everything's value. Asking yourself, "Keep, sell, donate, or trash?" may sound like a good first step, but it's not. That classification method would probably be easy if you were going through someone else's possessions, but it can be difficult and time-consuming to label your own things that way. Let's try a different exercise that may save you time and help put things into perspective.

Grab a watch, paper, and a pen and go to a quiet area out of sight from your home, like a park, café, or library. Leave your tablet, laptop, and smartphone behind so you don't get distracted or sneak a peek at your camera roll.

SPOILER ALERT: Leave your home before you continue reading in order to make the most of this exercise!

Now that you are out of your home, ask yourself, "If someone came in to repossess everything I own but gave me a chance to save one box of the things that mean the most to me, what would

I choose?" Take out your watch and time yourself. You have 20 minutes to list your most sentimental items, like something you kept from your wedding, a gift from someone who passed away, and the set list from your first concert.

Next, take 15 minutes to write down items you love, like your all-time favorite book and those jeans that fit unlike any you've ever owned before.

Finally, for 10 minutes, list everyday items you really want to keep, like artwork and electronics.

Your three lists include the first and most important things that came to mind. Before you head home, think about what didn't make the cut. Furniture? Kitchenware? The rest of your wardrobe? What do those things actually mean to you anyway? It's not that they're inessential, but they are replaceable.

Of course, the moment you walk into your home, you may see something you forgot to write down and want to scramble to add it to the list. Instead, use this exercise as an opportunity to acknowledge that you don't have to hang onto a particular material object just because you currently own it. If you didn't remember it while writing things down, you may not even remember it when you return from your travels.

Slow and sensible wins this race

The separation process won't be easy, and it's not a weekend project. What took years to accumulate will not take minutes to sort through and get rid of. It's neither a sprint nor a marathon, but rather something in the middle. Depending on your tentative departure date, you might have as long as a year to figure out what to do with your stuff. A year seems incredibly long, but the reality is that sorting through your possessions – the things you have a connection with and hold dear – can take a very long time. Still, you don't want to drag it out. If you don't keep moving, you may not finish before you leave.

 What it felt like to get rid of my stuff

It felt very freeing to pare down. I was happy to see it all go – until the middle of our final in-apartment sale. As I looked around at our kitchenware, my eyes stopped at my favorite French onion soup bowl. It was such a trivial thing, but it got me thinking about everything I loved to do and all the special moments Mike and I had shared in that apartment. He proposed to me in front of the IKEA bookshelf we were selling. As I continued to look around the room at the things we were selling, I got a little too nostalgic, and that was when the weight of everything hit me. It made me sad, but with any major life change comes sacrifice of some kind. I needed that moment to really let it all go and leave my system. Now, looking back, I'm very happy I didn't keep those things just because of the connection I had to them. I honestly feel more free and in control of my life now.

When you're ready to start actively going through your possessions, visualize how much storage space you'll have available. Will you fill half your parents' basement with boxes? A friend's spare bedroom? Once you know how much you're able to keep, you'll have a better idea of the amount you need to get rid of. And if you go a step further and anticipate having even less room available, you won't overfill your space when it comes time to stack boxes. If you do end up with extra storage space, you can always give last-minute reprieves to items that were on the cusp.

While we're encouraging you to downsize as much as possible, we know that not all of you will be able to reduce your possessions to just a few boxes – which is an understandably difficult thing to do. If you do need to rent a storage unit, ask for quotes from at least five locations in your area. Units in the suburbs or rural areas will typically cost less than those located inside of a city.

Even if you find that you need to rent a storage unit, the number of possessions you'll keep will more than likely be significantly smaller than what you currently own. That kind of downsizing will take a lot of time. Ease into it by devoting a couple evening hours after dinner a few times a week. Or even something as simple as paring down your wardrobe each morning as you look for an outfit to wear is a big step that will motivate you to continue. Once you get into a rhythm, devote additional time each week. This pace should also give you enough time to list and sell items, as we'll discuss soon.

Since you're starting to unclutter one year out, you'll have to be smart about what you get rid of first. The best items to begin sorting through are those that you don't use on a daily or weekly basis, but also not those hiding in boxes that live in the back of your closet. (You'll get to that back-of-closet stuff later.) Start with what is in open view around your home, like art, books, and decorative objects. We recommend beginning with these less-functional items because everyone tends to own a lot of them and they also sell fairly easily. (We provide tips for selling your possessions later in this chapter.)

If you are hoping to earn money from your book collection, for example, then you must start advertising them as soon as possible. It'll take a lot of time to list books individually and even longer for them to sell. Factors other than age and condition, like the beginning of a new school year, may affect their demand and therefore how quickly they sell. To give you an idea of the process, we listed and sold scores of our books (at least half of our collection) over the course of eight months. Even with our tireless efforts, we still didn't sell every book we listed and ended up donating dozens to charity.

 ## The great purge

I have had firsthand experience with emptying a two-story house, with an attic, basement, and a four-car garage that overflowed from decades of hoarding (my grandparents' home, not my own). Since both my parents and grandparents tended to collect things, I tried to avoid falling into the same habit. To me, moving was a great motivator. The more often I moved, the more often I had to pack, unpack and question the value of my possessions. It always made me feel like I should be shedding stuff, not accruing more things.

But finding the courage to enact a great purge is easier said than done. I had no compunction about tossing decorative items, but I had a lot of excuses for holding on to practical items. If I saw value in, let's say, a tool or device, I would keep it. The same went for any sentimental items. Letters, postcards, and anything else that had a personalized element, would be tossed into a box and kept – no questions asked. This was a sort of "off-limits" box that I would drag with me from new apartment to new apartment.

But our RTW trip really forced me to enact a more deliberate and controlled elimination. Instead of a frenzied panic, I saved only the things that really and truly mattered. It was bizarre to let go of items I had kept for decades, but this was a golden opportunity finally to throw these things away guilt-free.

In hindsight, I wish I had been able to do this sooner. Accumulating random possessions like shot glasses, picture frames, or tchotchke items was just weighing me down. By getting rid of these things before our RTW, I didn't have the desire to buy them as souvenirs while we were traveling.

Additionally, it has altered my post-trip perception of what I want to buy for our new home. We have decorations, but overall there is a practical vibe that comes from everything that fills the walls, closets, and living space in our new home. Things that I used to throw on a bookshelf or in a drawer and hold on to for no particular reason (like mail, birthday cards, and magazines I finished reading) are now recycled after I'm done reading or using them. It may have taken an RTW trip to shed the literal and figurative weight of unnecessary possessions, but I'm glad it did.

As you sort through these "non-essential" items, ask yourself, "Will I take this with me on the trip?" If the answer is "no," then you should ask, "Can I replace this easily and inexpensively upon our return?" If the answer is "yes," consider this item on the chopping block. Of course, it's good to ask more nuanced questions and weigh everything objectively, starting with an item's utility. But, ultimately, saving a less-meaningful item means that there won't be as much space for the things you need or truly care about.

Sorting through your "life," at least represented in material objects, is a highly personal task, which is why it can be very time-consuming and emotionally draining. If you and your travel partner do not live together, you'll have to stay focused and self-motivated when you're home alone. But since this is such a tedious process, it may be beneficial to bring in outside help to speed things up. Whether you can tolerate an outside perspective in this situation will depend on your personality, but don't underestimate the value in having someone else ask the hard questions. This will help put your possessions into perspective and ultimately help you get rid of things you can't bring yourself to part with.

Start organizing what you won't keep in one of three boxes labeled either "sell," "donate," or "trash." Setting up large boxes in your home is a visual cue that's hard to ignore. More importantly, it makes passive participation easy. If you see something that falls into one of those categories, even if you are not in the middle of cleaning, you can drop it in one of the containers.

Wrap up each week by emptying these three boxes. Advertise the items from the sell box. Bring the donation box to a charity or church, or give the items to friends. And don't forget to throw away the trash.

Once you finish sorting the less-functional items in your home, it's time to move on. Don't wait until all those things are sold, as it may take months for some items to leave your hands, and others may not sell at all. Your next focus should be on specific rooms. You may feel compelled to start with the bathroom since that seems like the quickest and easiest space to sort through, but don't. Choose a room that has items you know you want to sell or donate immediately.

The kitchen is a good area to begin. Many people, probably including you, have more cups, plates, utensils, and appliances than they use in a given month. You certainly don't want to get rid of everything this far out, but if you pare down now to just the essentials, you can use your last few months at home to focus on more important things than selling kitchenware. Plus, you might be able to make decent money selling your appliances and other items if they are in good condition.

You may be thinking, "But, won't I need pots and pans when I return?" Yes, they will be important to have when you get back. However, are yours brand new or so unique or expensive that they are worth saving? If not, this is your opportunity to make money for your trip. The cost to replace most kitchenware is minimal compared to the effort you must put into saving these unwieldy, heavy items. Size and weight are two important factors to consider when you're unsure whether to get rid of something. Storing too many boxes, especially heavy ones, will make you less mobile when you return and cause you to feel more overwhelmed when you are faced with unpacking everything.

After conquering the kitchen, think about which space makes the most sense to work on next. If you choose to clear out an armoire so that you can sell it, tackle it one shelf at a time. If an overflowing closet is next on your list but seems like too great of a challenge, take out a single container or stack of clothes and sort through it. Break larger rooms into smaller jobs and continue in this manner until you've sorted through your home. Clearing out just one closet might take weeks, but don't forget that this process is neither easy nor a sprint. And don't lose sight of why you're doing this. Keep the big picture – your trip and new life – in mind. If it helps, step away and stand in front of the world map you hung up. Smile, breathe, and keep going!

Make money while shrinking

Sometimes the easiest way to look at the things you own is in dollars and sense (no, that isn't a typo). If you are having a difficult time figuring out whether to keep something, think about how the profit may be put toward your trip. A three-course dinner for two in India: $5. A double room in a Malaysian hostel: $12. Entrance for two to the Hagia Sophia in Turkey: $25. Jumping into Devil's Pool in Victoria Falls, Zambia, for two people: $200.

The amount we earned from selling our household items funded one month in South Africa. That's right, an entire month of travel! This even included biking among wild animals through a nature reserve, cage diving with great white sharks, and the purchase of camping gear for an upcoming five-week overland safari. Had we known from the beginning that our profit would be so high, we would have pursued this task even more aggressively. Considering what the sale of our possessions allowed us to do, our strongest recommendation to other long-term travelers will always be to sell everything you can.

We took advantage of online marketplaces – like Craigslist and Amazon – that allow you to advertise your goods locally and/or nationally. Craigslist is good for large items that you wouldn't typically want to haul to a post office. Instead, you can indicate on your advertisement that the buyer is expected to pick up the item and present cash upon pickup.

Amazon is a more secure digital marketplace that will give you better success selling small one-off items like books and electronics (as opposed to a bookshelf or television). However, Amazon does take a percentage of your profit from items that sell, while Craigslist does not. The percentage is small, and they do reimburse you a flat amount for shipping (this is why you wouldn't want to sell and ship a large or heavy item – the reimbursement wouldn't cover the cost).

Additionally, all sales on Amazon are performed virtually (you never meet with a buyer and your profit is deposited directly into your bank account), while Craigslist requires in-person meet-ups for all transactions. This aspect of selling through Craigslist can make some people uncomfortable, so be sure to have a buddy with you if you have safety concerns and always meet the buyer in a public space during daylight hours.

Three steps and a tip for selling online

An easy way to part with some of your possessions while making money is through online marketplaces. This is what you should know:

1. First, note the condition of what you're selling – this directly impacts its value. Unless something is new and in its original box, do not expect to match the highest listed price or get top dollar for it.

2. Next, gauge the market to set a price. Amazon allows you to browse other sellers' prices, allowing you to set your item's value accordingly.

3. Finally, keep an eye on your listings. Give your items a deadline to sell. If you have not received genuine interest, lower the price accordingly. Sometimes the difference of a dollar will sell an item quickly or see it sit indefinitely. Repeat this process until the item sells.

Tip: Do not list an item on more than one e-marketplace where a transaction is immediately confirmed, like Amazon or eBay. You want to build positive seller ratings and reviews on these sites, and canceling a transaction because you sold the item elsewhere is frowned upon and won't entice the community to purchase from you.

Similarly, do not list your item on an e-marketplace and also host a yard sale or bring items to pawn shops and consignment stores. If an in-person transaction happens immediately, you won't have time to take your item off the e-marketplace. But you can put your e-inventory on "vacation mode" while you're trying to sell the items elsewhere.

If you want to list your DSLR in multiple places to increase its chances of selling, you have a lot of options in addition to choosing just one e-marketplace. Consider posting a classified advertisement in the local newspaper or on Craigslist.org. You can also hang flyers and send mass emails to friends and listserv groups. These types of advertisements are non-committal, meaning that if the DSLR sells on Amazon, you can tell an interested party who contacted you through email that the item is no longer available. If the item does sell through a classified ad, you'll have time to take the listing down from an e-marketplace before finalizing the in-person transaction.

Keeping digital copies and memories

Audiophiles and cinephiles will inevitably dig up unbelievable amounts of CDs, DVDs, Blu-rays and – dare we say it – cassette and VHS tapes. If this sounds like you, you actually might be in luck. Depending on the laws of your country and whether your music and movies are protected by anti-piracy software, you may be able to digitize the contents of your discs and tapes for personal use.

Like other things you own, it might make you sad to let go of the physical copies, but it will please you to know they can live on in an incredibly tiny and affordable external hard drive. Even though the digitizing and transferring process could take hours, having fewer items to store while you're away will make it worth the work (an external storage drive that holds one terabyte of information will take up less physical space than an average-sized book!).

 What is Digital Rights Management?

Most music and videos you purchase legally will have Digital Rights Management (DRM) embedded within the file(s). DRM is a digital roadblock designed to track the file and protect it from piracy.

Generally speaking, once you purchase a song from iTunes, for example, only computers authorized through your iTunes account can access this file, and this is also the case for video files. Legally, once you purchase a file, you're able to make as many backup copies as you desire, but the line is drawn when it comes to sharing with others, even family members.

But what about CDs, Blu-rays, and DVDs? What rights do you have when it comes to ripping digital files from physical copies of media you own? The easiest answer is: We cannot answer that question. Ripping media involves circumventing encryption, which may or may not be legal, depending on the laws of your country. However, know that digitizing your physical library for personal use does require you to still own the original copy of the media. You cannot rip your entire CD collection, keep the MP3s, and then sell the CDs to your neighbor. Some people believe that making files for personal use constitutes a fair-use exemption, but you should consult a lawyer if you are concerned or have questions.

One terabyte is a lot of digital space, but it is difficult to visualize. This chart should help put it into perspective (though keep in mind that data sizes will vary).

Content	Data Size	1 TB Storage Capacity*
1 digitized movie	2GB	500 movies
1 three-minute song	5MB	200,000 songs
1 medium-resolution photo	2MB	500,000 photos
1 minute of compressed video	60MB	270 hours of footage

*Approximate space.

As you can see, 1TB of space holds a lot of information, and that isn't even the largest size hard drive available. With so much space available to fill, consider digitizing other things as well — scan documents and photographs, compile personal videos you shot, download e-versions of books you like, and take pictures of objects you want to physically get rid of but keep as a digital memory. This is a great opportunity to organize and backup your life, digitally.

If you are concerned about storing everything in only one place, you can also research cloud-based backup services. The only drawback to this type of storage is that your access to it is limited to when you have an Internet connection. However, the upside is that if anything happens to your physical drive, you'll have everything backed up in the cloud and the ability to potentially access your account from anywhere in the world.

Henceforth, you may also want to consider purchasing movies, books, or music from Google, Apple or Amazon, as these companies allow you to access your files from anywhere in the world through your account, allowing you to stream or download the files according to your needs.

Even minimalists can downsize

This chapter has dug deep into the belief everyone has some possessions they can relinquish. But some people already feel as though they are living minimally. If you fall into this category, there is actually another step you can take: consider downsizing your home if you still have a year or more until your departure date. This applies specifically to those who are renting or those who feel they could easily rent out their home and pay less living elsewhere. If your space is currently larger than your needs, this is an easy way potentially to save hundreds of dollars a month and therefore reach your savings goal even quicker.

In our case, we moved into a studio apartment from a one-bedroom apartment about a year and a half before our departure date. This was prompted by the desire to save money (we paid approximately $400 per month less in the studio), but we were also able to make the change without compromising location or desired amenities.

We certainly lost space in the move, but this also forced us to take a proactive approach to downsizing our furniture much earlier in the process. We bid farewell to our couch and a few other bulky items that simply would not fit in our new and smaller space. Because we slimmed down our possessions prior to the move, our new home never felt cramped.

Many people may not be able to live in such tight quarters with another person, but remember that this won't be permanent, and it's a small price to pay for such a big monthly savings. You should also think of it as good practice for your trip, where you'll be moving from one small hostel or hotel room to another.

Making your final push

Even though we began selling items very early in our own pre-departure process, our biggest push to sell started five months prior to leaving. That's when we began listing furniture and other large items. We didn't want to package and mail them to buyers, so we advertised them online exclusively through Craigslist in order to have buyers come to us. Additionally, we hung flyers at work and inside our apartment building's elevators. And as our departure date crept closer, we held yard-sale style moving sales in our apartment. We were successful in selling a handful of items each week. Our profit would vary among items sold, but it was always encouraging to watch the money trickle in.

As you sell your possessions, track of your profits separately from your work income. This will give you a better understanding of your cash flow and show you how much your sales, in particular, are contributing to your savings goal. You can organize the information on a spreadsheet or hand-create a visual representation to hang next to your world map. One idea is to make a progress bar that fills up as you sell more. Mark off every few inches as $50, for example, and write next to it what that amount could buy on your trip. For example: $50 equals a EuroRail ticket. $75 equals a multiday trek. $100 equals a one-way flight. $200 equals a hot air balloon ride. As your progress bar grows and you see what your profits will buy on the road, you'll feel encouraged to continue the push to sell your things.

In your final week at home, after you've exhausted all profitable outlets, consider offering your remaining items to your friends and neighbors for free, including your kitchen pantry and liquor cabinet items. You could have an "Everything Must Go" themed party (you can even combine it with your farewell party). Tag items that are off-limits if you haven't finished packing. Give everyone a bag and cocktail when they arrive and tell them to fill the bag with whatever they desire. Everything they take is one less item you have to box up, throw away, or donate – it's beneficial for everyone (not to mention a fun send-off for you)!

Another option for offloading items during your final weeks is to ask a local charitable organization to pick up everything that's left. Many charities are not too keen on pickups unless it's for large items like furniture, but it's worth a try. Popular charitable options in the United States are Goodwill and The Salvation Army. Other groups that need and accept donations are schools, homeless shelters, non-profits, and religious organizations that disperse donated goods locally, nationally, and internationally. If you end up donating a lot of items, be sure to request a tax write-off slip for your donation. This may not amount to a significant savings, but every penny counts toward your trip.

While your profits may be high from the things you sold, you cannot solely fill your World Travel Fund just by selling off your possessions. You also need to properly save money, budget, and cut expenses if you want to depart with a healthy bank account and returning-home fund. We'll dive in deep in the next chapter.

CHAPTER IN REVIEW

❑ Change your attitude toward material possessions. If you never use it, lose it.

❑ Try not to let sentimental attachment prevent you from getting rid of stuff. A memory box full of childhood items is okay, but having 10 full boxes is too much.

❑ Reduce your possessions as much as possible so you have less to store while you're gone, won't have to rent a storage unit, and can have a fresh start upon your return.

❑ Ask friends and family to give you gift cards or make a donation to your travel fund instead of giving material objects for holidays and birthdays.

❑ Look into monetizing your possessions by selling them through online marketplaces and hosting a yard sale.

❑ Make digital backups of pictures, documents, or other memorable items and get rid of the hard copies.

❑ Downsize your living space to a smaller apartment to save money.

❑ Do not throw away worthy items that you can't sell. Instead, give them to friends and family or donate them to a charitable organization.

CHAPTER 3

The Cost of Travel and
How to Make a Budget
12 Months Prior to Departure

B Y MANAGING YOUR time, money, and energy in a more effective and efficient way, you'll reach your departure date faster (and more sanely). The key in this chapter is money. Once again, it will be vital to create attainable goals and set realistic deadlines to stay on track. Figuring out a successful game plan to save for your trip will require you and your travel partner to be honest about your finances and to stay honest about how you spend money after initiating your plan. Spending $30 on a nice meal may seem like a worthwhile splurge now, but just wait until you see what $30 could buy you in Cambodia! Now, let's start looking at ways to fill your trip's fund with some serious cash.

Reduce distractions

There is a failsafe way that will not only save you money, but will also limit distractions and help maximize your time. You probably won't like our suggestion, but we'll say it anyway: Cancel your cable subscription and sell your television. Whether you are actively paying attention to the TV or just have it on as background noise, it will be a distraction, plain and simple. The temptation to watch the latest movie, play videos games, or burn through an entire season of a show in a week will rarely win out against researching visa requirements and credit card options. The only true way to avoid being sucked into endless hours of flashing lights is to get rid of your television. Plus, selling it is a great way to add to your trip fund and decrease the amount of material items you'll put into storage while you're on the road.

Besides diverting your attention away from your RTW checklist, your television is impeding your progress even when it's not turned on. The money you were hoping to save to splurge on SCUBA diving in Malaysia is currently being spent on premium channels and electricity to power your flat screen. (Television sets use phantom power, meaning they are drawing electricity even when they are not turned on.) Doesn't seem like an equal trade-off, does it? The money you save by reducing expenditures like this will fund memorable experiences during your trip.

 Ask yourself the tough questions before you buy anything

When Tara and I first started to save for our trip, there was a month or two when I was uncertain which expenses to cut out. Without a savings goal in mind, I knew I shouldn't spend money frivolously, but what exactly did that mean? Did a bag of chips qualify as unnecessary? A soda? A cookie to go with lunch? It wasn't black and white to me at first, and a year is admittedly a long time to stop all unwarranted purchases. You don't want to just go cold turkey on all entertainment expenses, or change to a diet of beans and rice from here on out. What we needed was to set a goal, survey our habits, and then slowly decrease our unnecessary spending.

Once Tara and I created a savings goal, it was much easier to see exactly what we were working toward. In a way, we were micromanaging our finances by setting monthly, weekly, and daily savings goals, but these benchmarks also made it easier to track where our money was going. We started to recognize the bigger expenses that needed to be trimmed, like concerts, movies, and drinks at happy hour. While show tickets and weekend outings stick out as obvious splurges to cut back on, the "little" things you buy are the ones that fly under the radar and add up to kill your budget.

We saved receipts and Tara tracked where our money went. After looking at our weekly expenses, we decided to go on a spending diet, challenging ourselves every week to reduce or eliminate certain purchases. Instead of buying lunch at work, we started making larger dinners so we could pack the leftovers for the next day's lunch. Coffee was another large and daily expense that we decided could be cut. Well, not the coffee itself, but the hefty price tag. Instead of buying a $4 coffee every day, I invested in an inexpensive coffeemaker and the occasional $7 12-ounce bag of grounds. Within a month, the appliance had paid for itself, and over the course of the year, this adjustment saved us more than $1,000.

As you can see, little changes can surprisingly add up to big savings, especially for daily purchases. In most cases, you don't have to stop enjoying something, like coffee, but you just need to find a creative way to reduce the cost.

Often, you don't realize that you're making an excessive purchase. Maybe ice cream is on sale, but you normally wouldn't buy it. You have to think, "Is the extra $5 worth it?" Five such items in a single grocery run will quickly add up each week. So we devised a plan to help us whenever we needed to go shopping. Before heading to the checkout counter, Tara or I would ask ourselves or each other two simple questions:

1. For food or personal items: Do we just want it or do we truly need it?

2. For clothing, appliances, and the like: Can we take this with us on our RTW?

We were evaluating our purchases by being honest to ourselves about why we wanted them. I found that the simple act of asking these questions helped modify our spending habits by cutting down on impulsive purchases. Not only did this reduce expenses, it prevented us from accumulating items that later we would have been forced to sell or store.

Create a World Travel Fund with a savings goal

Before you can begin actively saving money for your trip, you must pay off your debt. You don't want to start your new adventure in the red. Make a plan to rid yourself of debt by listing out what you owe. Credit cards? Bank loan? Car payments? You can talk to a financial advisor for advice on how to pay them off, or initiate the snowball method of paying off the smallest debt first and working your way up from there. Another option is to organize your debt based on interest rate and pay off the one with the highest interest rate first.

If the only debt you have is from student loans, the good news is that you don't have to rush to pay them off. However, you should consider consolidating your loans if you haven't already. Before consolidating, shop around for the lowest rate, as many companies will be competitively vying for your business. These consolidation companies will entice you by offering a lower interest rate if you set up automatic bank withdrawals, versus paying by check. Doing this means you won't have to track several loans, and instead, you can have one manageable and predictable monthly payment that will be automatically deducted from your bank account. Just make sure you maintain enough money in this account during your trip so you don't have to monitor it closely.

We found ourselves in this situation (no outstanding debts except student loans) and made a plan a year prior to departure to ensure we wouldn't default on payments during our RTW. The plan included depositing a fixed amount from each of our paychecks into a particular bank account – let's call it our No-Touch Account. This account's specific purpose was for monthly student loan repayments before and during our trip. No other debits would be made from it. Eventually, our No-Touch Account held a dual purpose by also housing our return fund (money we would use to support ourselves after our trip ended until we could secure a steady income) since we didn't want to prematurely spend that money either.

To determine our savings goal for this dual-purpose No-Touch Account, we added two numbers together. First, the sum of the loan repayments we would make during a trip and for six months past our return (as a cushion should we not find work right away or decide to extend our trip). Second, we decided that our return fund would be equal to the average cost of living for six months, including rent, food, toiletries, and emergency expenses (see #5 in the following tips box for more details on how to calculate this number). The sum of these two amounts was our savings goal for the No-Touch Account.

Once you have your debt in order, you can begin depositing money into a World Travel Fund to be accessed during your trip. This fund should be in the form of a savings account that is separate from the No-Touch Account we mentioned earlier. Your World Travel Fund will be a deposits-only account until your trip begins. Like your other account, your fund needs a monetary goal, and not one to just work toward, but also past. (Having more money in the bank is never a bad thing!) And to determine your World Travel Fund's monetary goal, this brings us to the number one question on everyone's mind: How much does it cost to travel around the world?

The honest answer: It depends.

Here are some variables that could change the cost dramatically: where you go, how long you stay in each region, the type of accommodations you stay in, and what splurge activities you partake in along the way. Even though you may have a route and activities in mind right now, it could all change once you're on the road. You might fall in love with a city and want to stay longer. Your preferences could shift and you may opt for hotels over hostels. Any number of scenarios could change the cost of your trip, which is why you should always aim to save past your goal instead of just hitting it. Read through this next tips box to learn how to calculate a trip-specific estimate.

 Formula for determining a savings goal for your World Travel Fund

As a bonus for purchasing this book, we're providing you with downloadable checklists and worksheets that supplement this chapter and later chapters, as well as the expenses spreadsheet we used during our trip so you don't have to start from scratch. **Go to http://TwoTravelaholics.com/create-your-escape and type**

in the password TRAVELNOW to download the files. You'll want to use the Bucket List and Savings Goal files for this exercise.

Now we dive into the fun kind of math, which involves thinking about where you want to go and learning about how expensive or inexpensive it will be to travel there. The result of this exercise will answer the question everyone asks a world traveler: How much does it cost to travel full-time? You can even play around with the numbers until you land on an itinerary and travel style that will work with the amount of money you can realistically save prior to departure. Here is how to determine what your World Travel Fund savings goal should be:

1. Use your world map with pins to sketch out a rough itinerary. Six months in South America? Three months in Eastern Europe? Two months in Australia?

2. Research lodging costs. Find a booking website that you might use during your trip. Pull rates from the type of accommodations (that is, hostels, hotels, furnished apartments) you think you would stay in. Do this for the most expensive country or countries in each region you will visit. Multiply the nightly rate by the number of days you will be in that area to see what your total estimated cost of accommodations will be for that region.

Here is a practical example: You plan to travel in Southeast Asia for six months, or 180 days. Double-occupancy rooms in low-end Thai hotels range from $10-30 USD. The average hotel price we will use for Southeast Asia as a whole is $20. This number accounts for bungalows under $10 and splurges over $30. The accommodations cost for this portion of the trip will be $20 x 180, which is approximately $3,600 (this number includes both you and your travel partner, assuming you are sharing accommodations and expenses). This is just the cost of hotels for six months in Southeast Asia. Next you will calculate totals for the other regions you plan to visit and add them all together. The grand total is the estimated cost of accommodations for your whole trip.

3. **Implement the rule of three.** In theory, accommodations will be one third of your budget, excluding all pre-departure expenses. (This proved to be true for our 14-month trip.) Your next step is to take the total amount you approximated for accommodations in step 2 and multiply that number by 3. This new total is the estimated amount you might spend on accommodations, food, transportation (including long-haul flights), splurges, and miscellaneous purchases on the road.

Let's say you came up with $38,900. Do yourself a favor and round up to $40,000. Again, it's always better to overestimate, especially since you may not have a steady income during your trip.

Tip: To calculate your daily budget, divide the total by the number of days you expect to be gone. Keep this daily budget estimate in mind so you and your travel partner can use it as a guide for maintaining your overall trip budget while on the road.

4. **Account for a travel cushion and pre-departure purchases.** A travel cushion is that extra little bit you might need for unexpected expenses, additional splurge activities, or an added month in Indonesia. Pre-departure expenses can include travel and health insurance; immunizations and anti-malarial pills; new electronics like a laptop, camera, and external hard drive; and travel gear like clothes, luggage, and personal items.

To calculate this amount, take the total from step three (example being $40,000) and add 15% to it. Do this by multiplying that number by 1.15.

$40,000 x 1.15 = $46,000. This extra $6,000 should first be used toward trip-specific pre-departure purchases. The amount you have left will become your travel cushion.

And there you have it, the total amount you both will spend to travel around the world!

5. Make sure you have money when you return home. You should assume you'll spend every last cent of your World Travel Fund and therefore need a reliable cash source post-trip. This is where a return fund comes in (part of that No-Touch Account we mentioned earlier). While you could live with mom and dad for a bit, you want to prepare for the worst: monthly bills. It could potentially take months to secure a steady income when you return, and you may have to pay a cell phone bill and rent for an apartment while you wait, not to mention food, health care, and transportation costs (and don't forget those student loan repayments). This is why you don't want to return broke!

To determine how much you should deposit into your return fund, repeat steps two and three for where you hope to live upon your return. For example, does an apartment rental in that location cost $500 per month or $1,500? (Add in about 5-10% to account for inflation.) Multiply that number by the amount of months you realistically think you will be unemployed (and add in a security deposit and last month's rent just to be on the safe side). Now take that total and multiply it by three. This should give you enough money to return with. If you do have loan repayments, think about whether this cushion will cover them or if you will need to save more. This final number added to your World Travel Fund is your ultimate savings goal.

Take an honest look at your cash flow

Now that you have a savings goal, you must determine the best strategy for reaching it by your departure date. First, you have to understand your cash flow. To do that, take yourself back to high school algebra. Do you remember asking when and where you were going to use formulas again in your life? Well, now is that time. Treat your World Travel Fund as a formula. By plugging in your income, debits, and current liquid assets, you can easily determine how long it will take to hit your goal. In this next exercise, what you will learn about your cash flow will determine your spending patterns for the next 12 months. Consider this a high-priority task that you and your travel partner should start as soon as possible.

The first step is to break down your savings goal into a more manageable number, like a monthly target. Saving more than $20,000 in one year may sound like a daunting task, but saving $1,700 per month seems attainable. Since this chapter is all about numbers and math, we'll keep that trend going. The only way you'll know whether you're progressing toward your goal is to understand your cash flow. How much should you be saving per month ("A") compared to what you are currently saving per month ("B")?

 Income and savings are not even close to being the same thing

Think about what your yearly salary is. $40,000? $55,000? $75,000? It is easy to look at that nice round number and imagine that it will magically appear in your bank account each year. The reality is that your savings is not the same as your income. Every month, your paycheck takes a beating from taxes, social security, health care, your 401(k) contribution, and a variety of other deductions. Much of what's left of your paycheck will be spent on bills and personal expenses. The remainder is your actual savings. Without conscious and sensible money management, paychecks can easily come and go without adding a cent to your actual savings.

"A" is easy to calculate. What is your liquidity? How much of your liquid assets are you willing put toward your trip? Take that number and subtract it from your anticipated World Travel Fund savings goal. The difference is how far you are from your target (let's call that "C"). Divide "C" by the number of months you have until you leave, giving you "A." This is the amount you must save per month. Will it be easy or difficult?

The only way to put this number into perspective is to calculate how much you are actually saving per month, "B." Finding "B" is a three-step process. First, add your income sources together. Next, gather bills, credit card statements, and cash and ATM receipts to determine your monthly debits. Examples of what might fall into this category are payments for housing, cell phones, prescriptions, membership fees (if yearly, divide by 12), student loan repayments, as well as food, transportation, entertainment, and personal items. Compare debits month to month over a yearlong period to see if your spending has been consistent. This task is made easier by credit card statements, so this should not take long if you use a credit card often. If your spending varies widely each month, use the month in which you spent the most money to represent your monthly expenditures. It's better to overestimate spending than to use an average that may not account for unexpected high expenses.

Finally, complete this formula:

**Monthly Income - Monthly Expenditures =
Actual Savings Per Month ("B")**

Hopefully this produces a positive number! How does it compare to your goal, "A"?

If you calculate that $1,700 per month ("A") is your savings goal and $1,500 ("B") is your actual monthly savings, you still have to change your spending habits if your ultimate goal is to save $20,000 more than what you currently have in the bank. The $200 per month difference may not seem like much, but you are losing out on approximately $2,400 for the year, which is enough to fund a month's stay in many countries around the world. If you think about your daily expenses, you may be able to easily pinpoint items you spend too much on or can stop purchasing altogether. In one month, for example, you could save at least $200 by cutting back on eight cups of coffee ($4/cup), eight workday lunches ($8/meal), dinner and drinks at a restaurant ($25/meal), basic cable ($30/month), and going out with friends ($50/night). By reducing common expenses like these, you could easily pass your savings goal.

Achieving your goal requires patience, focus, and striking a balance between cutting expenses and not becoming a miserable miser. Ultimately, temptation will be your biggest hindrance to saving. If you know you have $8 in your wallet that you can spend on a workday meal, you may think, "Well, it's just this one time." Instead of giving into temptation, take steps so you don't find yourself in that position in the first place. In this example, the best solution is to pack a lunch the night before.

 Add another source of income

Everyone's monetary situation is different. Perhaps you think you can hit your monthly target by selling your possessions and reining in your spending. Or maybe you have to work extra hard to reach your goal by supplementing your income with a part-time job. I didn't necessarily think I needed a part-time job to help Mike and me reach our savings goal, but once I saw what a boost it was to our income, I was glad I had it.

I became a certified group fitness instructor about a year before we decided to take our trip. Every week, I taught three 45-minute fitness classes and made myself available to substitute other classes as well. Doing this made my days a little longer, but it was well worth the effort for the extra income it provided. I was working only two hours and 15 minutes more each week, but I adding $10,000 pre-tax to our household income. This part-time gig certainly proved to be an extra boost when we were really focusing on our savings. If you have the bandwidth to add a part-time job or accept freelance opportunities, you won't regret the added income.

Now that you understand your cash flow after completing that last exercise, the best way to ultimately nix temptation is to give yourself a pay cut. There are two ways you can do this. The first is to keep track of every penny you spend week to week. Write down how much you dish out and what you spend it on. Add it up at the end of each week. After a month, see when you spent the most money and what you bought during that week. Pinpoint unnecessary items you can cut out or down on (clothing, energy drinks, candy, cab fare). Then put yourself on a spending diet by cutting your week-to-week spending down by 25% or 50%. Challenge yourself by competing with your travel partner to see who can cut their spending by the highest percentage each week. Do this until you both are spending money only on absolutely necessary items. Don't forget: with sacrifice comes great reward!

 Budget for a social fund for your return

Friends and family will want to see you when you get back from your trip. Some of them will understand that your unemployed-and-potentially-homeless status means you aren't looking to spend a lot on an outing, but others may seem oblivious to your situation and urge you to meet for drinks, dinner, or join them at a concert. Additionally, you may come across a good opportunity to network over drinks or a meal during your job search.

You're going to want to see everyone, so you will most likely spend a bit of money on social activities. It's important not to go overboard and return to old habits of too many outings before you secure an income, though. Think about how much you normally spend on social activities now and, realistically, how often you might engage in one of these social activities when you return. Take transportation costs into account too.

When you determine how much you might spend per month, multiply it by the number of months you used to calculate your return fund. Finally, add 50-100% more. It's not that you can't trust your estimate, but you may be underestimating how easy it is to overspend when you're out having a good time. As always, we want you to over-save so your fund doesn't quickly vanish.

The other way to give yourself a pay cut is to literally reduce the amount of money you have direct access to. If the company you work for pays you through direct deposit, allot a fixed amount to be deposited into your World Travel Fund. This should be, at minimum, the number you calculated as your actual savings per month ("B"). Diverting this money to a no-touch account like your World Travel Fund will ensure that you spend no more than what you determined to be your maximum monthly spending. If you do increase the amount deposited into your no-touch account, you will have no choice but to adapt to your new income. This will jump-start your spending cutbacks and any creative money-saving techniques you implement. Finally, deposit the rest of your paycheck into an account that can be used to pay your monthly bills and personal expenses.

Just to recap, we have indeed suggested that you maintain three separate bank accounts. Your bank institution should not charge you to open additional accounts, and if it does, you should switch banks immediately. The first account is for your No-Touch Account (with your return fund and money for monthly loan repayments, if applicable). The second is for your World Travel Fund. Both of these should be treated as deposit-only accounts (minus loan repayment withdrawals). You can make deposits into both simultaneously or fill up your travel fund before focusing on your return fund. The third account will be used to maintain your current lifestyle and is the only one that should have both deposit and active withdraw activity.

Small cuts can lead to large gains

After moving through the exercises in this chapter, you may find that you will radically have to rethink your expenses if you want to depart on a certain date. Or, you may even be lucky enough to save for your goal while cutting back on next to nothing. Ultimately, making sound financial decisions falls on the backs of you and your travel partner. The key is to find what your income and your trip goal can support and then make sensible adjustments from there. Just remember that small adjustments to your lifestyle – daily, weekly, or monthly – will pay off immensely the longer you are able to maintain them.

CHAPTER IN REVIEW

❑ Cut back on your distractions, and start by cancelling cable and selling your television.

❑ Pay off your debt.

❑ Reduce or eliminate frivolous expenditures that are distancing you from your savings goal.

❑ Before buying anything new, ask yourself whether you can use it on your RTW or if it's an impulsive purchase.

❑ Calculate an estimate for what it might cost you and your travel partner to travel long-term according to your tentative itinerary.

❑ Understand your cash flow. Put your math cap on and create a realistic monthly savings goal for your World Travel Fund using your income and current debits.

❑ Create three banks accounts: a No-Touch Account, a World Travel Fund, and an account that will maintain your current lifestyle.

CHAPTER

Tips, Tricks, & Creative Ways to Save Money

FISCAL STABILITY IS the key to having true independence during your trip. More than just finding a way to stay ahead of your monthly bills, traveling long-term requires financial savings that will allow you to live without a steady income for the length of your trip, and then some. Reducing your spending is essential to achieving this goal if you're unable to add another income source. However, we know that identifying where you can cut back on your spending right now may not be so apparent. To help you jump-start your frugal mindset and lifestyle, we've compiled nearly 100 tips, tricks, and creative approaches to help you save as much of your income as possible.

Like any list, this is not a one-size-fits-all approach. Not every idea in this chapter will apply to your situation and, of course, you can't possibly implement them all overnight. Just like sorting through your possessions, it'll take time to break your habits and change the way you spend money. As you read through the following money-saving recommendations, give yourself two options for implementing the techniques: You can choose a few that seem less intrusive to slowly incorporate into your lifestyle or go all out and give yourself one heck of a challenge. Either way, you'll be amazed by how much you're able to save.

Free is better than cheap

Just because you're reducing your spending doesn't mean that new experiences and tangible goods are off limits to you. If you know where to look, you can find plenty of free products and activities around town.

1. Visit your local public library:
- Use the Internet and public computers.
- Read newspapers and magazines.
- Borrow books, e-books, CDs, and DVDs.
- Some libraries offer a service that allows members to download a few digital music files each week for free.

2. Take advantage of free museum entrance days. Once you're inside, join tours, group discussions, and other free activities and events they have on offer.

3. Find free community events through one of the following outlets:
- Read your neighborhood paper.
- Pick up an events calendar at the local library, city hall, or from the corkboard at a coffee shop.
- See if local performing arts theaters have free-admission performances or pay-what-you-can nights.
- Find open lectures or guest speakers at nearby colleges and universities.

4. Check out what your town's park and recreation board has to offer. You may discover free admittance to parks, trails, and rivers or canals, and free use of baseball fields, exercise parks, and basketball or tennis courts.

5. Pick up trial passes at gyms around town. Most gyms hand out day or weeklong trial passes to bring in new customers. No commitment is required, and you have free use of the facility for the duration of the pass.

6. Movie screenings aren't just for the media. There are websites that distribute free screening passes to the public. You not only can see a movie for free, you will also see it before its official theatrical release. Just search online for "free movie screenings" or "advance movie screenings" to see if they're available in your area.

7. See if the university you attended holds alumni events in your town, like panel discussions, networking events, or social activities.

8. Who needs a salon? Paint your own nails, give yourself a facial, straighten your hair, and test out home waxing. Haircuts are probably best left to the professionals, or at least professionals in training.

Reduce spending on necessities

Reducing your utility bills is a great way to save more money every single month instead of in one-off instances. You may find a few of these next suggestions challenging, but they're not impractical and are also generally good practices in conservation.

Even reducing your collective bills by just $10 per month will pay for a dip in Devil's Pool at Victoria Falls, Zambia. Maybe jumping into a natural infinity pool at the edge of a waterfall scares the bejesus out of you, but the essence of your trip is about conquering fear, and you can't begin to do that without enough money. Start by hacking away at your monthly bills with these tips:

9. Reduce phantom energy consumption. Even when they aren't in use, chargers and appliances draw power when they're plugged into an outlet. You have two options to help lower your electricity bill. One, you can plug in and unplug devices as you use them. Or two, you can keep your electronics plugged into power strips and then switch them on and off as you need them.

10. Using cold water to wash laundry will cost less per load than using hot water (think of the energy it takes to heat water). When your clothes are finished, hang them up to air dry instead of putting them in a drying machine.

11. Wet your toothbrush, and then turn off the tap while you brush your teeth.

12. When you clean dishes, fill the sink halfway with water. Scrub, scrub, scrub, then drain the water and quickly rinse the soap off each dish.

13. Master a three-minute shower. Pretend you are in a hostel shower that turns off every 15 seconds (these do exist!). Wet your hair and body, then turn off the water while you shampoo and soap up. Turn the water back on for just enough time to rinse off.

14. Swap out all incandescent lights for LED bulbs. LEDs are proven to use 85% less energy and have a longer lifespan.

15. Open your curtains and switch off lights during daylight hours. The sun is cranking out free light!

16. Allow fresh air inside. Open your windows and turn off your air conditioning. Maybe even turn on a fan instead. Think of it as practice for enduring the humidity in Southeast Asia.

17. In the winter, get cozy indoors by wearing layers and turning off the heat when possible. Otherwise, try not to turn up the heat as much as you normally would.

18. When you leave your home, turn off all lights, electronics, and the heat or air conditioning.

Try not to pay full price

Don't turn your nose up at coupons and discounts. Promotional codes for online purchases and even 50¢ coupons at the grocery store add up. Embrace these options for keeping more money in your pocket when you buy things you need.

19. Consider subscribing to your local newspaper if it runs a weekend coupon section (some free newspapers offer this as well). Weekend delivery service will pay for itself after using just a couple coupons. Scour the pages for things you need, like groceries, pharmacy items, and household supplies. Don't buy an unnecessary item because you see a coupon, but cut out coupons for products you typically use or need.

20. If you don't have a coupon or discount code for something you want, can you wait for it to go on sale? As long as you don't need something immediately, try to wait until it goes on sale or until you do find a coupon for it.

21. A sale at your favorite store may be enticing, but avoid going unless you actually need something there (to prevent spending money and accruing items unnecessarily).

22. Want to buy shoes for your trip? Before you get them at a brick and mortar store, check online first. There are websites dedicated to coupons and promotional codes that could save you even more money than an in-store sale.

23. Be a smart online shopper by using price comparison websites like pricegrabber.com to find out which website is offering the product you want for the lowest price.

24. Websites with daily deals and discounted products and experiences can easily turn on the "that's a great deal!" sensor in your brain. However, most offerings on those sites will likely be for purchases you are trying to avoid. Sometimes, though, you'll find great deals for things you need, like discounts on food that you would be purchasing anyway. As you stay on the lookout for relevant deals, don't forget to ask yourself if it's money well spent or money down the drain. It's also smart to compare the final sale price to other websites before making the purchase.

25. Look for first-time user discounts or rewards programs. Just by signing up, some websites might give you anywhere from $5 to $25 off your first purchase (who knows, maybe even more if you're lucky). This is free money! Since you'll be submitting an email address to sign up for these offers, create a separate email account for instances like this so you don't have to unsubscribe from dozens of email blasts on your main personal account.

26. Visit a professional in training. If you want a deep discount, go to a cosmetology school to get a haircut and a dental school's clinic for reduced-cost fillings or procedures that may not be covered or covered fully by your insurance.

Become a master of the grocery store

Technically, you can buy everything you need online. While Internet shopping may help you reduce impulse purchases, you'll likely still need to head to a local grocery store. Supermarkets are full of temptations, making them the perfect place to test your self-control. If you want to walk out with a shopping cart and receipt you'll be proud of, you need to go into the store with a plan.

27. Write down what you want to buy and make sure all items are necessities. When you get to the store, stick to this list 100 percent.

28. Question the things you in your shopping cart, even if they are on your list. Do you do you typically pay extra for a certain brand? Ask yourself why and if it's a necessary habit to continue.

29. Stop before you hit the checkout line to make sure you didn't add in any impulse or excessive purchases. Gourmet olives? We know it's difficult, but put them back. When you visit Istanbul they will be a quarter of the price in the local bazaar, not to mention fresh instead of canned.

30. Buy in bulk. If you eat eggs and yogurt for breakfast every morning, buy the family-sized carton of eggs and a large tub of yogurt. You know you'll use it before the expiration date because you eat it frequently, and you will definitely be saving money. Here are some other items you can consider buying in bulk:
- Produce. Purchase whole foods since pre-sliced fruits and vegetables are overpriced and have a shorter lifespan. Also, instead of buying just a few potatoes at a time, buy a five-pound bag if you know you'll use it.
- Grains like rice, bulgur, oatmeal, quinoa, couscous, and popcorn
- Dried beans
- Nuts

- Flour
- Trash bags
- Laundry detergent
- Hand, body, and dish soap
- Shampoo and conditioner
- Toilet paper
- Napkins and paper towels

31. Don't overspend on hygiene and cosmetic products. Paying a premium for toothpaste, face wash, and lotion can be a major expense. Find products with the active ingredients you need and buy the cheapest ones.

32. Purchase generic medicine when possible, as generics will always be cheaper than brand-name drugs. To gain government approval in the United States, generic drugs are supposed to be bioequivalent to the brand-name drug it is imitating (you can read more about this on the U.S. Food and Drug Administration's website). Therefore, next time you have to pick up a prescription or over-the-counter medication, purchase the generic equivalent of what you need.

33. When you're at the supermarket buying food or toiletries, purchase store-brand products when possible. Check the ingredient label on packaged foods to see what you're consuming, as ingredients aren't required to be the same as the popular equivalent.

Let your creative juices flow

Don't forget to have a little fun with this money-saving adventure that you're on. Use these ideas as a starting point to think of other creative ways to challenge yourself while saving money.

34. Test your self-control by making weekly or monthly resolutions that drive down costs:
- Cut out meat or go vegan. You'll save a lot of money by not purchasing meat, eggs, and other dairy products. Your health will thank you too!
- Make it yourself. Instead of buying pasta, consider making it at home from durum wheat and water. Homemade polenta is easy, too. All you need is cornmeal, water, butter, and salt. Try your hand at baking bread with flour, yeast, salt, and water.
- Skip juices and sodas.
- Cut out drinking alcohol.
- Walk or bike to work instead of driving or taking public transport.
- Choose one day each week when you are not allowed to spend any money at all. Start with No-Spend Saturdays, and then expand to No-Money Mondays.

35. Eat less meat. If going full-on vegan, vegetarian, or pescetarian is too difficult, just cut back on meat. Participate in Meatless Mondays and reduce your meat consumption for the rest of the week. When you do eat meat, have smaller portions so your purchase lasts longer.

36. Spend more time in the kitchen and less time at restaurants and fast-food eateries. You'll save a lot of money by making home-cooked meals more frequently. Double the recipe so you have leftovers for the next day's lunch or dinner.

37. Make homemade vegetable broth by saving the trimmings from your produce (like the tops of carrots, mushroom gills, tips of celery, and herb stalks). Each time you would normally throw away a piece of produce, put it in a bag that you store in your freezer. When the bag fills up, dump it into a pot, add some water, and simmer for 45 minutes. Then drain the broth into glass jars and store them in your fridge.

38. If you bought whole or bulk produce that you won't be able to use before it spoils, freeze it for later use or add it to your vegetable broth pot.

39. Eat breakfast at home and bring lunch to work instead of purchasing it at a quick-service restaurant.

40. Skip the vending machine and bring your own snacks to work. Easy options: fruit, popcorn, trail mix, cheese with crackers, and veggie slices with hummus.

41. Set aside a couple hours on the weekend to make extra-large portions that will feed you through the week. Think stews, stir-fries, curries, pasta bakes, casseroles, and slow cooker meals. Freeze what you don't think you'll eat that week and store the rest in multiple containers that you can easily pack for work or reheat for dinner. Plan these large dishes based on what's on sale in the Sunday circular, not based on a particular recipe, as ingredients from a cookbook may be expensive or not on sale.

42. Buy popcorn kernels and cook them on your stovetop for a light and cost-effective snack instead of purchasing overpriced microwavable bags.

43. Got leftovers or a bunch of oddball items in your fridge? Play "Ultimate Cooking Challenge" by finding a way to repurpose leftovers or combine random ingredients in your fridge to make a new delicious dish. Here are some ideas:
- Make soup. It's filling and economical and arguably one of the best ways to use your leftovers since you can combine almost anything with herbs and spices to make a tasty creation.
- Stale bread: Pulse in a food processor to make breadcrumbs.

- Rice-based leftovers: Ball up your leftovers with an egg, breadcrumbs, and additional spices to make rice balls, or flatten them out to make patties. Bake and enjoy!
- Leftover meat or vegetables: Add to curry, baked pasta, spaghetti sauce, omelets, sandwiches, burritos, stir-fry, casseroles, soups, or salads.
- Leftover pizza: Get creative! Use it as a bread base for a casserole or frittata.
- Too much chili? Transform it into sloppy joes. Put it on top of rice, polenta, a hot dog, or a taco. Do as the locals in Cincinnati do and top your spaghetti with chili and cheese.
- If you have fruit that is overripe, bake a pie, blend it into a milkshake, or freeze it and then add it to a smoothie.

44. Throw a potluck to try new recipes, see friends, and not foot the bill for the entire party. Maybe you'll even be able to keep some leftover food for the next day's lunch and dinner.

45. Start a garden. If you're not leaving for a while, buy plants to cut down on produce expenses at the grocery store. A $4 tomato plant will produce many tomatoes for months and in the end cost less than buying tomatoes at the store. Not to mention the fresh, homegrown taste!

46. Instead of using paper towels to clean or wipe down surfaces, cut up old T-shirts and use them as rags that you can wash and reuse.

47. Use cloth napkins instead of paper.

48. Water down juice to make it last longer.

49. Splurge now to save later. If you have poor eyesight, consider getting Lasik or another corrective procedure. This will cut out the cost of glasses, contacts, and lens solution, as well as make life easier on the road when you take overnight transportation or if you break your glasses or run out of contacts or solution.

50. Do you have a problem with your shoes? Instead of purchasing a new pair, have them fixed by a cobbler for a fraction of the cost.

51. If you rely on your car to take you around, keep it well maintained to help you achieve better gas mileage. This means keeping your tires inflated, changing the oil when it needs it, and getting regular checkups to ensure the engine is working at maximum capacity.

52. Rent out unused space in your home. You could host travelers through booking sites geared toward homestays, like AirBnB. If you have enough room for a tenant, consider finding a renter for your basement, extra bedroom, or guesthouse.

53. Downsize your home by renting a cheaper space. If you own a house and plan to sell it before your trip, do so as soon as possible. Clean it up, get it appraised, and find a realtor. Then search for a house or apartment to rent for a lower monthly payment.

Cancel, reduce, and cut out

By its very definition, a habit is a practice that is difficult to alter or end. If you enjoy buying a bagel from your favorite bakery on your way to work every morning, it might be difficult to break that routine. You need something to replace it that doesn't make you feel like you've lost a special part of your day. If you want to change your spending habits, you essentially have to create a new routine and mindset. Keep that in mind for this next set of recommendations.

Cancel your...

54. Gym membership. Instead of dishing out money every month, exercise outside, play workout DVDs at home, utilize free public recreation areas, or start collecting and using free trial passes to local gyms.

55. Subscriptions and memberships. These might include magazines, newspapers, online games, online video or shopping sites, wine of the month club, and season tickets for a professional team.

56. Cable. Instead, borrow DVDs from friends, stream TV shows and movies online for free, or check out movies from the local public library.

Reduce your...

57. Cell phone plan. Evaluate your monthly bill and cancel services you don't use or opt for a cheaper plan. Even moving from unlimited data to 4GB per month will save money. Better yet, if you can survive without a smartphone, cancel your plan and purchase a prepaid phone that you only use for emergencies. If you are under contract with your current plan and will be penalized, calculate whether the savings is worth canceling the plan.

58. Internet usage. Consider whether you need an Internet package at home as well as a smartphone with a data plan. Free WiFi hotspots are becoming much easier to find, and you can even use Internet for free at public libraries. If you do need a connection in your home for work or another important reason, consider changing your package to a cheaper option.

59. Coffee consumption. Even a $2 cuppa joe each day adds up to

$730 each year. That could buy you a one-way flight between two continents. It's difficult to just eliminate a habit like coffee, so try to train your taste buds to enjoy espresso or black coffee instead of a double-the-price latte or cappuccino. Better yet, invest in a French press and buy bags of coffee grounds so you can brew your own at home for a fraction of the price.

60. Transportation costs. It's expensive to maintain a vehicle, and if you have one you'll need to think about what you'll do with it while you're away. We recommend selling it and then using these alternative methods of transportation:

- Walk or bike as much as possible.
- Take public transportation more often.
- Carpool with neighbors or coworkers.
- Sign up for a ridesharing program.
- Combine errands or do them during or on the way home from work so you don't make multiple trips.

61. Vacations large and small. Cut back on these to save for your bigger trip. If you want to head out for a holiday weekend, go on a road trip where you pack a cooler of your own food and drinks and camp or visit family and friends for a free place to stay and to see them before you leave.

Cut out…

62. Unhealthy snacks. Grazing on food all day can add up to be an expensive habit. Help your wallet and your health by nixing things like sweets and chips from your diet.

63. Sodas, juice, and/or other sugar-laden drinks. Instead, drink more water. You can add citrus or cucumber to water for flavor or buy inexpensive tea packets to make pitchers of tea. This will also prepare you for your trip because water will be the cheapest and most ubiquitous drink around.

64. Drinking alcohol at bars. It's tough to just drink water at happy hour when your friends are enjoying an alcoholic beverage. To ease yourself in, try watering down your drink, sipping slowly to make a drink last as long as possible, or drinking a full glass of water in-between each alcoholic beverage – but slowly.

65. Expensive habits. Smoking, drinking, drugs, gambling, and playing the lottery are a few examples.

66. Purchasing bottled water. Instead, buy a reusable bottle that you can refill with potable tap water. If you don't like the size of the hard-plastic bottles, you can buy one that is made of a flexible material that can flatten and fold to fit in your bag, purse, or pocket.

67. Buying sealable plastic sandwich bags and instead purchase reusable sandwich bags. These eco-friendly alternatives are sealable, come in different sizes, and can be washed and reused.

68. Conditioner. You may think this is odd, but you might stop using it during your trip. It adds more weight to your pack and takes up precious space. Try to make conditioner a treat you use once a week or consider buying a 2-in-1 shampoo plus conditioner product. (Note: this is something Tara started doing during our RTW trip and still continues now, years later.)

Financially speaking

Use your current savings and job-related perks to your advantage before you leave your job. Here are a few ways to maximize your time and your dime.

69. Research all the benefits of your job and use them before you lose them. You may not even realize the wide array of perks you have, so consult your human resources department to obtain a full list. Ask about the following:

- Discounted lawyer and financial advisor services. Have a lawyer create a will, living will, and power of attorney if you do not already have those set up. Since your trip revolves around you being able to afford to go, it is a good idea to discuss your financial options with a professional advisor.
- Discount on cell phone plans through certain providers. You may get 15% off your monthly bill just by letting your service provider know the company you work for.
- Free or reduced-price software or electronics.
- Free access to educational courses or e-tutorials that can teach you skills for your trip. These might include blogging, web coding, foreign languages, and photography editing.

70. Talk to a financial advisor about the best ways to store or invest your savings. It could be as simple as discussing a CD (certificate of deposit), money market account, the stock market, or a retirement fund.

71. If you don't need to talk to an advisor but want to research basic financial information, there are free websites that can help. For example, Bankrate.com has data to help you compare rates (bank and automotive, for example), calculate your debt, research credit cards, and more.

72. There are free financial management tools online, like Mint. com, that chart your credits and debits for a more holistic view of your finances. Before linking your accounts to an online site, always thoroughly investigate its legitimacy and level of security.

73. Give yourself an automated pay cut. For each paycheck, funnel a certain amount of money into a no-touch savings account (like your World Travel Fund). Doing this will help you save more and learn to live on less.

74. Whenever you pay for a purchase in cash, keep all coins you receive as change and store them in a jar at home. When the jar fills up, deposit the money. You'll be pleasantly surprised by how much you were able to save.

75. Make more money. Consider a part-time job or on-demand work opportunities (freelancing, brand promotion, dog walking, and even babysitting) to add to your income.

76. Volunteer for paid studies at local universities or research centers.

77. Pay your bills online with a credit card. Besides being more environmentally friendly, you don't have to pay for a stamp, and by using your credit card to pay bills, you can accrue points and earn rewards.

78. Finally, pay for as much as you can with a credit card that earns you the most points for every dollar spent. If you don't already have one, compare cards based on how many points it takes you to earn $X cash back, products and services, or free flights or hotel stays. Figure out which is the best one that you qualify for, and then apply for it and use it as often as possible.

Start now and stay motivated

As we said in the beginning, putting these ideas into practice can be much easier said than done. But if you and your travel partner support and encourage each other, it will be less stressful. Try to find a silver lining and turn these challenges into a friendly competition. Whoever spends the highest amount each week or month (excluding necessary bills) has to cook for the other person for a week. Or set a monthly savings goal for you both to reach, and whoever doesn't reach it has to take on household cleaning duties alone. Think of ways to motivate each other, even if it means splurging once at the end of every month on a nice night out if you both meet your goal. Even though we don't want to encourage any pre-trip splurges, sometimes you need a few to stay motivated.

Being creative while staying focused will help keep you track to save, while not compromising your lifestyle. These money-saving recommendations are only the tip of the iceberg. There are websites and books dedicated to thrifty living, and we encourage you to read them to find other ways to save more and spend less. Strive to identify potential small changes in your behavior that can add up to larger savings over the course of a year or longer. By adjusting your habits now, you are not only helping to fund your trip and make it a reality, but you are also making a long-term lifestyle change that will continue to affect the way you spend money long after your trip ends.

CHAPTER 5

Where in the World Will You Go?
9 Months Prior to Departure

IF YOU HAVE been implementing each chapter's recommendations without jumping ship, then congratulations – you are officially committed to the idea of an RTW trip! The first steps of setting goals, reducing possessions, and cutting spending are the most difficult and perhaps least exciting. But by overcoming tough challenges at home, you are ensuring that you can conquer anything when you are out of your comfort zone abroad. We had to hit you hard with reality to see if you are worthy enough to continue. You obviously are, so keep the energy up and let's start having more fun!

Draw up your ideal route around the world

This is where the fun begins! It's time to tighten up your tentative

RTW itinerary. Think outside the box as you look over the map you hung on your wall. What experiences will elevate this trip from an ordinary vacation to a once-in-a-lifetime opportunity? Do you want to be a passenger on the Trans-Siberian Railway? Eat authentic Indian food? Go on safari in the Serengeti? Join in on a giant tomato fight at La Tomatina? Write down every event, attraction, and experience that you've ever dreamed about. Be adventurous and include places you have never visited. Think big and don't limit yourself – you can refine your list later. If you consider this to be your one chance to fit in everything you've ever wanted to see and do around the world, your trip will be action-packed and truly unforgettable. Embrace the saying, "Live every day like it's your last."

If the number of possibilities leaves you unsure what to actually pursue and what to cut, think about your goals for the trip and what you want to return having done and learned. Are you looking at your trip as an opportunity to volunteer your skills and time? There are programs all over the world that accept international volunteers and some even offer free room and board. Is there a cuisine you love that you want to learn all about? You might decide to spend months in Malaysia so you can take culinary classes around the country. Perhaps you want to become bilingual? Research language-immersion programs. The flexibility of long-term travel offers you the chance to stay in a location for more than just a couple days or a week. Likewise, the longer you can commit to learning a new skill or offering your time as a volunteer, the more it will enrich your life.

Settling down for several months in a foreign country may not be what you envision for part of your RTW, but you can change your travel dream list at any time. (As you revise your itinerary while you're still at home, recalculate a travel budget estimate for these new locations and adjust your savings goal accordingly.) In fact, it would be ideal for your route to remain flexible even once you're on the road. You may arrive in a country where the culture shock hits you so hard that you would prefer to leave immediately. On the flip side, you may decide to visit a country that you learned about from other travelers while on the road. And there are always unexpected and unfortunate reasons you may have to take a detour, like illness, civil unrest, or natural disasters like earthquakes and typhoons. The more flexible and patient you are through changes and challenges, the more positive your outlook and experience will be.

Once you finish creating your travel wish list, read over it and on another piece of paper write down which countries you will need to visit to achieve all of your location-specific and non-location-specific goals. Create a visual representation of your potential route around the world by reorganizing the pins on your world map or printing another map and highlighting the countries you want to visit. After you mark your chosen countries, decide which direction you want to travel and how long you might stay in each country. Finishing these last steps will actually help you do more than just achieve a potential route. This information will help you pack, apply for visas, fine-tune your budget, determine which immunizations to get, and more.

 Time to tell Mom and Dad

You've been downsizing, saving more money, and plotting out a tentative route, but now it's time to think about your family. Letting your parents in on your trip, if you haven't already, can be kind of nerve-wracking. For me anyway, telling my Mom and Dad that we were going to leave everything behind to travel the world wasn't easy.

To understand why, you have to know that my parents always encouraged me to do well in school so I could get a great job.

I graduated at the top of my class at university, and then after graduation turned an internship into a job at one of the most prestigious newspapers in the country. They had an idea of what my future should be, and my path appeared successful in their eyes. I knew that this trip, with all the risk and uncertainty that it entailed, wouldn't seem like a wise career move to them. But Mike and I had already made our decision – we were going to do it!

When we were hip-deep in pre-departure preparation mode, I found out my parents were coming into town in September 2011. It would be a great opportunity to tell them about our trip in person even though I was nervous to do it. They've always been supportive, but I knew they wouldn't react well to, "Mike and I are going to quit our jobs to travel around the world after we get married." My parents are logical people, and I knew they would think we were crazy if I presented the trip without a concrete plan around it. My biggest fear was that they wouldn't support us.

There were a few things I did to help me through the talk. I started by calling the trip our "extended honeymoon." Mike and I were going to get married in March 2012 and fly out a couple months later, and since we were planning the wedding and trip at the same time, it seemed appropriate to label it as our honeymoon. I thought this phrasing would help soften the news and make our decision seem more like an opportunity instead of an impulse.

Besides framing the trip as an extended honeymoon, I wrote up talking points that I wanted to cover. These notes were very helpful for me when it came time to tell my parents as well as other people. My outline started off very basic, "We have some great news to tell you. We are taking an extended honeymoon and traveling around the world. We will start in May or June and be gone about a year." Then it went on to explain the reasons we were excited to take the RTW trip and why now was the perfect time for us to do it. Then

I moved to the "how" and explained our planning process and our goals leading up to departure. This proved that we had spent time planning this, and it wasn't an ill-thought-out decision. Additionally, I also threw in some inspirational quotes about the importance of living the life you want, mostly as additional motivation for myself. I loosely followed these talking points when it came time to talk to my parents, and having the outline definitely helped prepare me.

Approaching the big talk, I used my notes to practice a little with Mike to prepare for various scenarios. Although my parents were usually supportive of my decisions, I knew they would not let such a major life decision go unquestioned. I had to be prepared. Practicing helped me navigate through the conversation with more confidence.

The last thing I did to help this chat with my parents go smoothly was to make sure that other family members, who I thought would be thrilled for us, would be around. Their audience turned out to be an asset, as they seized on the trip's excitement, and we were able to parlay that energy into keeping the conversation positive.

As a result of all my efforts, the talk ended up going better than I thought it would in some respects. It really helped to mentally prepare for any reaction, as it's very difficult to predict how some people will take your news.

In a later chapter, we'll talk about how and when to deliver the news to friends, your boss, coworkers, and the rest of the world. For now, it's best to tell only your very closest friends and family members – but hold them to secrecy!

The importance of drafting a tentative itinerary

Just like every other part of the pre-departure stage, it's up to you how much effort you want to put into researching and planning. Believe it or not, some people prefer to close their eyes and let the wind blow them around the world. We never want to discourage spontaneity, but there are good reasons to have at least a tentative route in mind.

Vaccinations are a perfect example. When you visit a travel nurse, you must tell him or her where you plan to go, how long you will be there, and which activities you hope to participate in. This information helps the nurse determine which shots you need. If you decide to forego this important step, you may not be able to travel as freely as you hoped.

The yellow fever virus, transmitted by mosquitoes, is a good example of this. The yellow fever virus exists in tropical South America and sub-Saharan Africa. Not only should you protect yourself against the virus by getting the vaccination, but if you travel in a yellow fever zone, subsequent countries you attempt to enter will require you to present your yellow fever vaccination card. If you cannot show proof that you have been vaccinated against yellow fever, you will be denied entry into the country. Situations like this require you to plan ahead, or you might miss out on an exciting opportunity.

Similarly, you should know which countries on your wish list require a visa for entry. We suggest doing a bit of this research now because you won't be able to get all your visas prior to leaving home. Visas have an expiration date, some as short as three months, so it's important to know what your options are.

At this point in the planning, you don't have to worry about details such as the cost of the visa or what the application process is like. Instead, research the following two things: whether the countries you want to visit will grant citizens of your nationality a tourist visa and if it will be possible for you to obtain all required visas on the road. Cross any country off your list that will not grant you a tourist visa because of your nationality. If you are allowed to enter the country, find out whether a tourist visa is required (you don't always need one). Some countries require you to obtain the visa prior to entry, but others offer a visa on arrival (VOA). If a country doesn't offer a VOA, you'll want to know if you can apply for the visa at an embassy or consulate in another country. (For example, if you're traveling from South Africa to India, you'll want to find out if there's an Indian embassy or consulate in South Africa.) You may come across embassies or consulates that don't distribute visas at all, but maybe there's another in a different city that does. And sometimes you'll discover that there isn't even an embassy or consulate for your next destination in the country you're currently visiting. Be sure to jot notes from this research next to each country on your map.

 What is a visa?

A visa, plain and simple, is a sticker applied to a passport page that grants the traveler entry into a specific country for a certain amount of time. Not all countries require a visa, though. Whether you will need one depends on your nationality, the purpose of your visit, and which country you plan to enter.

There are many types of visas (such as tourism, student, business, and temporary worker), and you must apply for the one that best describes the purpose of your visit since the category will designate your status and limit the activities you can (legally) participate in while in the country. For example, some countries require an employment visa for volunteer work, so you wouldn't want to apply for a tourist visa even if you plan to volunteer for only a couple weeks.

Each visa type does cost money. Sometimes when cash is the required, they may ask for the payment to be in a foreign currency that isn't used for everyday commerce in the country. In these cases, unless you came prepared, you'll simply need to go to a bank or currency exchange.

There are a variety of ways you can obtain a visa, and some countries might give you multiple options while others only offer one. Often, travelers wanting a tourist visa can purchase a visa on arrival (also known as a VOA) at an international airport or a port or land border crossing. Some countries have even implemented an e-visa system that allows you to apply entirely online and virtually link the visa to your passport number. Others will require you to submit an application in advance of your travels, typically at the country's embassy or consulate or sometimes through an outsourced company.

Whenever you fill out an application form for a visa, you are usually asked for your basic contact information, your current employment situation, the length of your stay, which cities you plan to visit, and an address you plan to stay at while there (this could just be a hotel you might book). Applications also require one or two passport-sized photos and, sometimes, proof of onward travel (an outbound flight confirmation), proof of adequate funds (a bank statement to show you can buy a ticket out of the country), or sponsorship from a school, employer, or tour agency.

Tip: We brought passport-sized photos with us so we wouldn't have to scramble to find a shop that sold them.

If you're really lucky, you won't need to apply for your VOA at all. Depending on your nationality and the country you enter, you may just need to pay a small sum of money for a small sticker before crossing through the immigration line – and that's it!

Aside from visas and vaccinations, knowing which countries you might visit will give you time to research more than just the top 10 things to see and do. Think about what information might be essential to know to help you have a more positive experience. This can include researching travel advisories, electrical outlet plug type and voltage, the local cuisine if you have a food allergy, and the average cost of transportation within and between cities.

During our RTW trip preparation, we did thorough research for only the first few countries on our itinerary. We stopped short due to time constraints, but we were hopeful that we'd have the ability to do research later. As we traveled, we found there were countries on our itinerary that we wished we had researched early on. It would have been helpful to know, for example, that many nations adhere to a conservative dress code. Often, we rushed to buy appropriate clothing, like pants or sleeved shirts, once we realized our faux pas. Locals will sometimes say they don't expect foreign tourists to dress in the same manner, but by covering up we avoided uncomfortable stares. We quickly learned that a simple search prior to entering a new country wasn't going to cut it and that we needed to ask different questions and more questions to avoid surprises like this one.

 Make a list, and check it twice

World travelers should always be respectful of other cultures and knowledgeable about the countries they visit. Some of this will be acquired through immersion once you're in a new location, but a wise traveler will educate himself or herself prior to arrival. To help boost your world knowledge, start by researching these questions for the countries on your itinerary:

1. What is the official language? Are secondary or tertiary languages widely used as well? How do you say hello, goodbye, thank you, one, two, and three? What are some other useful phrases?

2. What are the local customs, etiquette, and taboos? This can include how you greet another person and what not to do while eating.

3. How conservatively do locals dress? What are their expectations of foreign visitors?

4. What is the local currency? What is the going exchange rate? Are credit cards widely accepted or will I need to obtain cash?

5. Are gratuities a customary practice among locals? If so, when is it appropriate to tip and how much?

6. What is the current season and average temperature? Is there a "better" or "worse" time to visit throughout the year?

Doing such research is also an opportunity to discover reasons to visit a country or city, and not cross it off your list. After all, you are traveling to learn and experience new things. Read as much as you can about the local culture, language, etiquette, and weather patterns so you are more knowledgeable about your travel options and also prepared when you arrive.

Plan a route that will save money

In the last tips box, we asked whether there is a "better" or "worse" time to visit a country. Typically, a country's high or low tourism season is tied to weather. Weather like heavy rainfall, extreme heat or cold, or snow (unless you're headed to a glacier or ski resort) will usually cause a drop in the number of visitors, making it low season. If you don't mind such adverse weather conditions, traveling during low season certainly has its perks. There are fewer tourists, shorter lines, and reduced prices for hotels, tours, and activities. Unfortunately, you also run the risk of encountering reduced or canceled transportation options since the demand is lower. Hotels and restaurants also may be closed for the same reason or for seasonal repairs or upgrades. But with a little extra planning and knowledge of what to expect, adding a few low season months to your long-term travel plans will reduce your overall costs and give you a different experience than if you went during the height of tourism season.

Invest in the international community and reap the benefits

Early in planning process, we looked into money saving options for when we would be on the road. Most of these opportunities revolved around accommodations that were either offered for free or in exchange for work since we knew that accommodations account for one third of expenses. One of my responsibilities was to look more closely into how we could take advantage of these networks.

From the outset, I wanted to avoid "pay-for-play" websites that required a monthly or annual fee to join. It struck me as odd that you would have to pay for a service that other sites offer for free. Still, I researched all of our options by reading reviews and blog posts about the various sites. Ultimately, I found there were three main categories for discount accommodations:

1. Housesitting sites (Trustedhousitters, MindMyHouse, Caretaker) charge for access to their listings, usually monthly. You're required to have a detailed profile and personal and professional references. You have to be able to sell yourself over the competition if you want the keys to someone's house while they're out of town. For the majority of housesitting opportunities, you'll typically secure a gig weeks or months in advance, and dates aren't flexible since they hinge on when the owners will be out of town.

2. Volunteering sites (WWOOF, HelpX, Workaway) can charge or be free. These sites also require extensive profiles since you're essentially applying for what is usually a limited number of open spots. The businesses that are members of these sites are typically more flexible with dates since you may be required to apply for a temporary work visa in order to volunteer.

3. Homestay sites (Couchsurfing, BeWelcome, AirBnB) do not charge a subscription fee. Some of the sites are essentially homestay booking engines, so you can expect to pay on a per night basis much like a hostel or hotel. Others have more of a community feel and don't charge. Filling out a thorough profile on these sites are for your benefit, though not a requirement, as many members will accept your request either way.

Couchsurfing (CS) was the most appealing to both of us. First, it's free, and you can't beat the price. Second, you get to stay with a local, see how they live, and pick their brain about the area and what to do. Third, it gives you the opportunity to meet a like-minded person and potentially become friends. Being part of this community appeared to have the most benefits.

When we first discovered CS, we were living in a studio apartment so we could save more money for our trip. Our space was so small that we would need to rearrange the furniture to accommodate a queen-sized air mattress for any guests. Becoming hosts before our trip didn't seem like a good option for us – or any traveler. Luckily, we found out that local CS hosts planned events that allowed you to be involved in the community without requiring you host others. Since we wanted to learn more about what type of people would let strangers into their homes free of charge, we started to attend some of these meet-ups.

After attending a couple CS events, we became more comfortable with the community and wanted to know more. We soon learned that your virtual presence meant far less than the reputation you created through meeting up with other CS members. After hanging out with, staying with, or traveling with another CS member, you could write a reference for them that would appear on their profile, essentially vouching for their character and letting the community know what kind of person he or she is. Positive testimonies usually translate to hosts accepting your requests.

Getting involved early in Couchsurfing or BeWelcome is crucial if you are hoping to use these sites during your trip. If you don't have a well-defined profile or any references, you may find fewer people willing to host you. The overwhelming majority of Couchsurfers we have met are generous, caring, and friendly people, but it is harder to persuade someone to host you if you have not been active in the community.

Start building CS relationships while you are still at home, even if it just means showing a visitor around your city or taking them out to coffee. Beyond having a reference, this could also lead to a close friendship or a future host for you and your travel partner. Being well connected within the travel community could lead to other introductions while you're on the road too.

Beyond offering their homes to you, we found that our hosts were usually seasoned travelers themselves. They were often thrilled to share tips and recommendations. I found these interactions to be incredibly informative and rewarding. Not only did these conversations help create a more intimate experience in these locations, but they often left us with additional recommendations for destinations we would have otherwise missed.

And finally, I don't know about you, but in my mind, free is always a plus.

Another way to reduce costs while traveling is to use overland transportation instead of airplanes. Flying is the best option when you want to get somewhere faster and without stopping along the way, but flying between all or even most of your destinations will kill your budget. If you have the time and desire to travel slower, you can better enjoy the scenery and all aspects of the journey. We decided to take a 26-hour bus ride from Luang Prabang, Laos, to Hanoi, Vietnam, instead of a one-hour flight that was three times the cost. It was a difficult decision because we were eager to get to Vietnam and didn't want to spend any more time driving on Laos' windy roads. But in the end, we were glad we opted for the bus. Yes, it saved us money, but the ride wasn't so bad (actually kind of comfortable), and now we have a fun travel story to share with others.

Also, when you opt for experience over convenience – like a bus versus plane – you become a valuable resource for others who wonder which option is best. Most flight experiences are pretty similar, but people will ask you questions like, how was the ferry ride from Morocco to Spain? Where did you purchase tickets? Would you do it again? Having that kind of knowledge will differentiate you from other travelers in addition to making your experience special in its own way.

 Being a good [Couchsurfing] host

We felt a little odd entering the Couchsurfing community as surfers instead of hosts. It usually shows good manners when you give a little before taking a lot. Unfortunately, our manners weren't well developed yet. But we did learn a lot from our hosts about how to be good hosts, mostly because it's human nature to critique experiences, and Couchsurfing was no different for us. There were things we loved about our hosts: they showed us around, let us extend our stay, and cooked traditional dishes for us to share, to name a few. And of course there were a few things that went well but could be improved upon, like setting expectations up front.

Now that we've surfed more than a dozen times and have hosted people ourselves, we feel better suited to give advice. If you are interested in hosting a traveler or two prior to your departure, think about these tips for being a great host:

1. Accept the type of guest who is right for you. When you open yourself up to host, think about the kind of person or people you want to invite into your home. Someone who makes it clear they're only looking for a place to sleep? Or do you want to host someone who is hoping to interact with you? Review the requests you receive and also take a look at the surfers' profiles and references to get a feel for who they all are and how they interact with their hosts. Request to Skype if you want to ask them questions or build rapport before they arrive.

2. Set expectations up front. What is the maximum number of nights they can stay? Do you allow smoking in your home? Should they always remove their shoes at the front door? Do you want your guests to clean any dishes they use? Will you give them a set of keys or should they leave in the morning by the time you head to work?

3. Be direct. While some people might take "make yourself at home" to heart, others may be timid and need you to be more explicit. On their first day in your home, tell them whether they can do things like use the laundry machines, eat food from the fridge, and connect to your Internet.

4. Give them space but be available. Traveling is exhausting and sometimes it's nice to be in someone's home. Let your guest zone out if that's what they want. When they're ready to be active and social, spend time getting to know them, whether it's talking over a meal or showing them your favorite local spot.

5. Make memories. Do something nice for your guest that will help elevate their experience. Maybe you take a day trip together or give them a walking tour of your city. If you have a car, pick them up from the airport or drop them off at an attraction on your way into work. Invite them to hang out with you and your friends. Whatever you decide to do, make it special.

The key to being a good host is treating your guests how you would want to be treated. Think about the annoyances of traveling and try to eliminate them for your guests. Brainstorm fun ways to introduce a visitor to your city and play tour guide. And don't forget that while some people surf for the experience of staying with a local, others may feel burnt out and need to decompress, and perhaps they feel most comfortable doing so in a home instead of a hotel. Let them relax if that's what they want to do, and don't judge them for it.

Choose a route that will also lighten your luggage

During your trip, your life will be contained in one, maybe two pieces of luggage. The size and weight of your bags will certainly affect your physical and mental well-being while you're on the move, so you definitely want to avoid packing too much. One of the easiest ways to pack lighter is to avoid the season that requires additional layers and bulky clothing – we're looking at you, winter! The travel route we recommend is to hemisphere hop and chase an endless summer around the world. By continuously traveling in warm weather, you will shed the need for bulky winter clothing items like gloves, scarves, thermals, and a thick coat. (You can always purchase items on the road if you come across an opportunity that takes you into cold weather.)

Aside from carrying lighter luggage, an endless-summer itinerary will help you avoid delays and cancellations due to snowfall (rainfall is another matter, especially on islands). Getting snowed in at an airport can strand you with thousands of others who had an outbound flight – a definite damper on your plans. Acts of nature, like adverse weather, generally absolve airlines from any responsibility to their passengers, which may leave you searching for last-minute accommodations, canceling and rebooking future plans, and more. You should embrace any opportunity to dodge such unfavorable situations.

If you do decide to follow an endless summer, you'll need to remain cognizant of the weather. As it starts to cool down, you and your travel partner will have to change hemispheres to get back to warmer weather.

 ### How we decided which direction to travel

We were nine months away from departure, and we hadn't yet figured out the exact date we would leave, where we would begin, or the direction we would travel. Choosing our first destination was important because it would allow us to finalize our departure date (by taking into account which month we wanted to leave and when airfare would be the cheapest) and our options for where to go next. With a world map spread out on the floor of our apartment, we each chose the top countries we hoped to visit. After many discussions, India, Iceland, South Africa, and Thailand topped our list, so we examined their locations and tried to figure out an optimal and efficient tentative route.

Mike came up with the idea to travel on an endless-summer path, which promised warmer weather and lighter luggage throughout our trip. By doing this, we wouldn't carry around cold-weather clothes that would go unused for months. We would only have to pack for warm weather (and the occasional cooler night) and just be sure to switch hemispheres as the seasons changed.

Our goal was to leave the United States in June, the beginning of the Northern Hemisphere's summer, which gave us a foundation for considering various routes that would take us through our top bucket-list countries. The only wildcard was Iceland. Summer is the only time visitors can see most of the country, as many roads are closed outside of these warmer months. We hoped to drive around the whole island, which meant that we had to visit during June or July. Therefore, Iceland had to be either our first or last country since we planned to travel from June 2012 through July 2013.

It may seem like a no-brainer that we would make Iceland our first stop, but the rest of Europe wasn't on our itinerary for two reasons. One, we had previously backpacked extensively through the continent and wanted to visit new destinations. And two, we wanted to travel at length through Asia and Africa since overland excursions aren't ideal to do during a week or two off work. So we thought of beginning our trip in Asia in June 2012 and making Iceland our final destination in July 2013, thereby traveling around the globe in a westward direction. However, Iceland is an expensive country to travel in, and we were worried that we may not have enough savings left by the time we landed. On the other hand, if we made Iceland our first stop, we would travel eastward around the world and stay in the Northern Hemisphere until September or October before moving south. We just weren't sure where to go after Iceland since the rest of Europe wasn't on our itinerary.

After many discussions, we couldn't find any convincing benefits for visiting Iceland at the end of our trip, and we definitely didn't want to cross it off our itinerary entirely. Ultimately, several reasons persuaded us to choose Iceland as our starting point:

1. We really wanted to go. Iceland was one of our top bucket-list countries, so we definitely wanted to fit it in and didn't want to risk cutting it out at the end of our trip.

2. Plane tickets were actually inexpensive. At the time, Icelandair offered low fares to Keflavík from the east coast of the United States, and also out of Keflavík to mainland Europe. Since we weren't traveling round-trip, we bought two one-way tickets each (to Iceland then onto Helsinki), and our combined fares ended up being cheaper than a one-way ticket straight to mainland Europe or to Africa or to Asia.

3. We could visit Europe afterward. Yes, we did previously say we wanted to skip the rest of Europe during this trip, but of course there are countries we hadn't visited, so we decided we would spend the rest of summer and fall in Europe before heading south to Africa.

4. We could pack specifically for Iceland. Iceland Air allowed each of us to check two bags for free. Iceland is still cold in June, so instead of purchasing new clothes at the end of our trip, we wanted to take advantage of the airline's checked baggage policy. We filled an additional suitcase with warm clothing (that we would have otherwise gotten rid of prior to leaving DC), a tent so we could camp, and packaged food to help us save money while there. At the end of our stay in Iceland, we donated our extra luggage to our Couchsurfing host and her daughter instead of throwing it all away.

5. We would arrive during shoulder season, when low-season prices are still in effect. Our research told us that transportation and accommodation prices in Iceland dramatically increase from June to July. Traveling there first gave us the opportunity to begin our endless summer while saving a bit of money since we had planned to return home in July of the following year.

6. We didn't want to freak out about paying higher prices at the end of our trip, especially if we arrived in Iceland with very little left in our World Travel Fund. We knew Iceland was going to be pricey, and it was by far the most expensive country we visited. By starting our trip there, we wouldn't yet have a point of reference for the cost of things in other countries. Even though every purchase we made – from hotel rooms to meals – seemed expensive, we still hadn't been exposed to Southeast Asian prices. If we began our trip in less expensive countries, we would have felt guilty about spending so much in Iceland and may have tried to cut corners, which could have drastically changed our experience.

By deciding to go to Iceland first, we reduced our overall costs by finding creative ways to save on food, airfare, winter clothing, accommodations, and a rental car. You can see we put a lot of thought into it, and you should also consider similar ideas when thinking about where to start your trip so you can optimize your spending.

Another thing to consider is that heat can bring the potential for other types of unfavorable conditions. For example, you may arrive in Southeast Asia toward the end of the dry season. During this time, farmers use slash-and-burn agriculture on their fields for regrowth because the dry landscape can support controlled fires. Some call this the burning season. The slash-and-burn technique usually renders the air smoky, difficult to breathe, and poor for pictures. This time of year is followed by the rainy season, which, as evidenced by the name, is when torrential rains occur (though some days you may see only an hour or two of rain).

This sounds like a less-than-ideal time to travel, and you'd think that the region would receive few tourists during these months, but this is actually not the case. In an ironic twist, we were in Southeast Asia from February until August and found fringe benefits to traveling during this time. For one, the rainy season is considered a shoulder season – not exactly high or low – so a lot of activities and transportation options, like seasonal ferries, were still open and available. Rates for activities, accommodations, and transportation are sometimes half of the high season rates. Also, the seasons are different depending on where you are within the region and even which side of a country you're on, so you may be able to dodge it. This is where your pre-departure research comes in. Check the weather and write down when the seasons occur so you can keep them in mind while traveling.

Buying an RTW ticket versus individual segments

After you sketch out a tentative itinerary, you should consider whether to buy your long-haul flights individually or purchase an RTW ticket ahead of time. An RTW ticket is essentially a multi-destination ticket that can be purchased from airline alliances, like OneWorld and Star Alliance, or third-party travel agencies, like STA Travel and AirTreks. This may be a good option for those who are particularly budget-conscious since you would know up front how this high-priced item (essentially all of your long-haul flights) will affect your budget. Others may enjoy the convenience of booking all these flights in one fell swoop before departing instead of piecemeal on the road.

Booking flights from the comfort of your home beats trying to find secure Internet access on the road, but convenience comes with a price. When purchasing an RTW ticket, you must submit a firm itinerary that cannot be changed without incurring a hefty fee, though dates and times may be changed for free. This is a good option for anyone who wants to have a set schedule so they can plan their RTW in detail. Additionally, you must complete your itinerary within one year of the original departure date, follow a single direction around the world (east to west or west to east), and adhere to the alliance's rules regarding movement within and between continents.

Besides being a smart purchase for travelers who have confidence in their route, airline alliance-issued RTW tickets are also ideal for those who want to enjoy the benefits of loyalty programs. Since RTW tickets are created using partners within an alliance, you can accrue miles that count toward elite status and can also be exchanged for free tickets or other perks.

If you plan to travel for more than a year, you won't be eligible to purchase an RTW ticket from an alliance, but booking through a third-party agency is another good option. Instead of simultaneously booking all segments within a single airline alliance, your travel agent will search for the lowest-priced combination airfare for your route. Since airlines typically don't open their reservation system for flights that are 11+ months out, third-party agents patiently wait for your remaining segments to become available and then book them even after you leave home. Unlike the alliances, these agencies don't have rules preventing you from changing route directions or going back to the continent you previously came from, which gives you more flexibility with your route. You might not gain elite status by going through a third-party agency, but you may end up paying less.

While this sounds more accommodating than an alliance-issued RTW ticket, it actually ends up being less flexible after the booking is completed. To subsequently change times, dates, or destinations, you must pay a fee. The reason is that your agent actually books your ticket when you settle on a flight, unlike the alliance, which just places a hold on your spot. In order for agencies to secure the lowest price, they typically purchase non-refundable tickets. So depending on the change you want to make, they might have to completely cancel and rebook the ticket, which could cost quite a bit. Sometimes you may luck out and find that your reason for changing dates is covered and approved by your travel insurance, allowing for a partial or full refund. This is something you'll also want to keep in mind when choosing a travel insurance provider.

Another advantage of an RTW ticket versus buying individual segments is the level of service that comes with it. By purchasing an RTW ticket through one agency or alliance, you will have access to customer service representatives who will take care of everything after you submit your itinerary details and credit card information. Simple things like applying for visas can become even easier. Since some visa applications require you to submit proof of onward travel, having an RTW ticket means you'll never have to scramble to purchase a flight at the last-minute.

There are certainly a lot of benefits in purchasing an RTW ticket, but inflexibility is the biggest drawback. Personally, we didn't like the thought of being "locked" into a timeline and set route. So we ultimately chose to purchase individual segments as we traveled. This allowed us to move at our own pace, staying longer if we loved our location or moving on if we felt the urge. During our pre-departure planning, our original route had us traveling to each continent except Antarctica. Once we were on the road, reality set it. It was not possible to follow our dream route, unless we rushed from country to country. Since we enjoyed the pace we were traveling at, we decided to completely skip Japan, Australia, and South America rather than force them in. If we had an RTW ticket dictating our route, we would've either made costly amendments to our flights or tried to keep pace with the pre-planned itinerary – neither an optimal situation.

Another drawback is short-haul flights. You'll likely end up buying a few as you travel. RTW tickets are intended for long-haul flights, and while domestic or short "hopper" flights can be included, you'll end up spending more money to include them in the ticket because RTW tickets don't use budget airlines, like Ryanair or AirAsia. You would save money if you purchased these as individual one-way tickets outside of your core RTW ticket. You may think now that you will find other ways to travel between departure cities, but you might later discover that the overland route is notorious for being hazardous – maybe because of landfalls or poorly paved roads – and you would like to avoid the danger by flying to your next destination instead. Additionally, if you're on a tight schedule, you'll definitely save time by hopping on a one-hour flight instead of taking a 24-hour bus. And, surprisingly, flights through budget airlines can sometimes be cheaper than a train, ferry, or bus. Long-term travelers with flexible schedules will often be able to find such deals because of timing or a fare sale. But the cost of these last-minute flights will be in addition to the cost of your RTW ticket, making the final cost of all flights higher than you originally thought. Be sure to keep this in mind when you're thinking about your transportation budget.

As we mentioned, we didn't purchase an RTW ticket. Out of a total of 15 flights, we purchased four before we left our home. The remaining 11 flights were purchased on the road, and often a month or less from our departure date. We watched ticket prices fluctuate but held off purchasing until we felt confident with the date and location and, most importantly, were pleased with the amount of time we spent in a region before moving on.

Another factor that sometimes affected our decision to fly instead of enter a new country via bus was the type of visa we would receive upon arrival. For example, we spent almost $200 on two last-minute flights from Penang, Malaysia, to Phuket, Thailand, so that we could get a 30-day visa instead of the 15-day visa some nationalities are granted by entering overland.

 ## Breakdown of real-life flights without an RTW ticket

Take a guess. What do you think two people spent on 15 one-way flights over the course of 14 months? Don't cheat by reading on. Take a second to think about both long-haul and short-haul flights around Europe, Africa, India, and Southeast Asia. Ok, now we'll tell you that we spent approximately $7,400. That totals around $3,700 per person.

Keep in mind that flights won't be the only thing eating up your transportation budget. We actually spent $2,841 per person on all other types of transportation, which includes buses, minibuses, taxis, trams, trains, ferries, bicycles, subway tickets, donkey rides, a horse carriage, a mokoro, safari truck, tuk tuks, songthaews, motorbike taxis, water taxis, and a rental car plus gasoline. Fortunately, walking is free!

Not only will drafting a tentative RTW route help you create a budget and savings goal, but knowing where you might travel will also help you more accurately compare prices between an RTW ticket and the total cost of individual flight segments.

If you are interested in seeing how an RTW ticket stacks up against individual flights, use our trip's totals on the next page as a guide for comparison. All monetary values are listed in U.S. dollars. (Don't forget that each segment includes two tickets. For example, the $200 USD total from Mandalay to Bangkok was actually for two $100 USD one-way tickets.)

Flight path	Cost (2 pax)
New York City, USA, to Reykjavik, Iceland	$629
Reykjavik, Iceland, to Helsinki, Finland	$322
Helsinki, Finland, to St. Petersburg, Russia	$231.94
Moscow, Russia, to Istanbul, Turkey	$355
Istanbul, Turkey, to Zagreb, Croatia	$292.52
Zagreb, Croatia, to Dubrovnik, Croatia	$113.26
Milan, Italy, to Casablanca, Morocco	$349.90
Lisbon, Portugal, to Cairo, Egypt	$445.40
Cairo, Egypt, to Johannesburg, South Africa	$889.40
Dar es Salaam, Tanzania, to Kolkata, India	$1,318.50
Kochi, India, to Singapore	$269.03
Penang, Malaysia, to Phuket, Thailand	$191.66
Bangkok, Thailand, to Yangon, Myanmar	$189.10
Mandalay, Myanmar, to Bangkok, Thailand	$200
Ho Chi Minh City, Vietnam, to Virginia, USA	$1,614.40

When we compare the "ideal" route we drafted before we left and our eventual path, there is little deviation aside from the amount of time spent in each region and eliminating our final few destinations that we simply no longer had time to visit. We were also able to squeeze in countries that we didn't originally intend to travel to, like Malaysia and Myanmar, which were recommendations from expats or fellow travelers. Otherwise, we stuck to the destinations we were most interested in visiting and had researched.

Drawing up a tentative route now will not lock you into anything yet, and the benefits are abundantly clear. Knowing destinations you might visit will help you research RTW tickets and individual flights, as well as visas, vaccinations, weather, and important cultural information. Preparation will never hurt your trip or chances for spontaneity; it will simply educate you so you have more knowledge with which to make decisions. Now get to work, and let your excitement push you to places you would never visit on a normal two-week vacation!

CHAPTER IN REVIEW

❑ Write down your top bucket list cities, festivals, events, and experiences.

❑ Can you obtain a visa to visit all the countries on your list?

❑ Get involved with international communities before you leave your home. Like-minded travelers are a great resource for information and can potentially connect you to others during your journey.

❑ Don't underestimate the value of planning an endless summer trip.

❑ Weigh the pros and cons of buying an RTW ticket versus individual flight segments.

❑ If you drastically change your route or add expensive destinations, be sure to update your savings goal accordingly.

CHAPTER

Before You Leave, Learn...
6 to 3 Months Prior to Departure

A S YOU'VE COME to see, long-term travel requires a different kind of preparation than the average two-week vacation. That's because you're actually setting the foundation for a brand new life. During your trip, you'll encounter situations you will never face at home. They may cause you frustration, like not understanding local language, or lead to a missed opportunity, like not being able to go on a day trip because you don't know how to drive a motorbike. The situations may vary, but it is easy to foresee one thing: being as prepared as possible will make you a savvier traveler.

Preparation also requires having a good idea of what the road will toss at you. We know you're already insanely busy paring down, cutting your spending, and working on cost-effective itinerary options, so we're providing you with some suggestions of things to work on that will help you become a heads-up traveler. You may not see the value in some of them right now, but you will once you're on the road, and the longer you travel the more some of these situations will recur.

If you are indeed traveling with someone else, you can skirt by without having to learn everything. Take advantage of there being two of you and use your time effectively by dividing and conquering new skills or responsibilities. For example, you both don't need to know how to stitch up a torn seam or sew a button back on, but one of you should. Assign the task of being the trip's emergency tailor to one person even if it means they need to learn sewing techniques. Of course, this wouldn't be something to start learning six months out; it can definitely wait until closer to departure. Other things, like swim lessons or using chopsticks, won't fit into the divide and conquer theme and will also need to be learned and practiced for months instead of at the last minute. We'll give you a rundown of some typical situations that travelers encounter, and you can determine their importance based on your and your travel partner's current skillsets and desires.

Life skills you can conquer in a few months
6 months prior to departure

Some skills won't take more than a few days or weeks to pick up, but others will require enrolling in a class, taking tutorials, and practicing for months. For classes, you may be at the mercy of seasonal enrollment and may miss the window if you wait too long. Teaching yourself isn't always as effective, so for the following topics, start looking into classes at least six months before your trip begins. Then you should feel comfortable with your progress by the time you depart.

Start learning another language

English is everywhere. It is widely spoken and used in signage all over the world. While we as English speakers certainly have our own moments of difficulty on the road, we discovered that English is shared by far more people than other languages. There were myriad situations when we saw non-English speakers struggling to find a common language to communicate in with locals. Its accessibility makes English a great language for international travelers to know.

While we were fortunate, we never took this for granted and always tried to learn the dominant written and spoken language of the countries we visited. This took a lot of practice and often we were just starting to master a few words or phrases when it was time for us to leave the country. This is why we highly encourage you to learn a language before you leave, especially if you plan to be in a certain country for weeks or months.

Even just learning the basics of a language (like common phrases and how to pronounce letters or characters) will help you immeasurably when you arrive. This attempt to speak in the local language will often endear you to locals. We found that people were almost always friendlier if we used a simple greeting and tried to communicate with them in their native tongue. It always helps break the ice and improve any situation.

 Alternative ways to learn another language

It can be intimidating to start learning a new language, especially if the last foreign language course you took was in grade school. Some people thrive in classroom environments, and if this describes you, then you can consider taking a night class or auditing a college-level course. If not, take the pressure off yourself by stepping out of the classroom with these fun alternatives:

- Use a computer-based language program like Rosetta Stone®.
- Check out books and audiotapes from the public library (they're free!).
- Find someone who knows the language and is willing to help you practice.
- Look for local groups that meet to practice the language. The added benefit of this method is that you may learn more about the country and culture from others in the group.

While language classes are great for learning the basics, especially if you're only starting six months prior to departure, the best option would be to enroll in an immersion program once you're in-country since it really forces you to sink or swim. The only issue is that this isn't an overnight option and is typically a commitment of a couple months. However, the major benefit is that you will likely walk away with better fluency than you would through other means. If you choose this option, you should still start studying the language at home. Doing this will give you a basic foundation to use once you arrive in the country, as well as better position you to learn more advanced parts of the language during your program.

Learn how to drive

Yes, literally. If you don't have recent or any experience driving a motor vehicle, now is the time to learn. You not only should be comfortable driving, but you also should make sure you have a valid driver's license once you hit the road. Renting a car and driving yourself is the only way you'll have full independence and control of your trip, especially if you want to visit destinations that public transportation and tour companies don't go to. For example, we rented a car and drove around Iceland's Ring Road and were able to take myriad detours along the way. Plus, doing this gives you the opportunity to travel at your own pace instead of following someone else's timeline.

Knowing how to drive an automatic-transmission vehicle is great, but it's even better to feel comfortable with a manual-transmission vehicle too. Manual cars are very common around the world (though automatics dominate in the United States), and many car rental agencies offer them as a lower-priced option to automatics. If you don't know how to drive a manual, start practicing now, as the process is very different from driving an automatic and will take you some time to learn.

Feeling comfortable with a manual transmission will go a long way in avoiding stressful situations on the road. For example, you may be faced with having to drive on the opposite side of the road from what you are used to. This means not only having heads-up awareness to properly shift your vehicle, but also ensuring you are following the country's rules of the road. It can be a lot to handle, so being prepared for the unexpected is important, and also the theme of this chapter since we don't want you to pass up any opportunities due to lack of preparation.

If you plan to rent a car, you should also know how to change a flat tire. Road tripping across a populated area makes it easy to flag down a Good Samaritan or call for help, but what if you're in a remote location? Even if your rental comes with roadside assistance, there's also the possibility that your phone dies or can't pick up a signal. Worse, what happens if you can't walk to get help? You or your travel partner should know how to jack up the car, detach the damaged tire, and screw the spare tire securely into place. Additionally, knowing how to change coolant or troubleshoot basic problems can be vitally important as well.

Practice driving a motorbike

Just as you'll find many manual-transmission vehicles around the world, motorbikes and scooters are king in some regions. If you want to rent a vehicle in a country like Laos, for example, a four-wheeled vehicle won't be an option. Instead, you'll likely be choosing from a manual, semi-automatic, or automatic scooter. Most guesthouses rent out motorbikes by the day and offer beat-up helmets as well.

Driving a motorbike is risky in itself, no matter how skilled a driver you may already be. But if you haven't ever driven a motorcycle or scooter, we strongly encourage you to take lessons prior to departure. Doing so will teach you defensive driving, the basics of how to handle the bike, and how to operate manuals and semi-automatics. Speaking from experience, we tried to teach ourselves on the road and walked away with some cuts and bruises, and saw many other travelers with casts. Again, it's better to acquire these skills before you leave in case you don't want to pass up an opportunity to rent one or, heaven forbid, an emergency happens and you have no choice but to get behind the wheel.

Before you sign the rental contract, you may want to look into how corrupt the local police are. In some countries, foreign tourists are viewed as ATMs, and you may be stopped and asked for bribe money. If for some reason you have no choice but to rent a vehicle in a location like this, come up with a plan for how you might react should you find yourself in this situation. Being calm and levelheaded instead of nervous, worried, or confrontational will help the situation end quicker. Typically, police will claim that you lack the proper documentation for driving in that country. One such document is an International Driving Permit (IDP), and while it's not a necessary document in all countries, it is worth the money and effort to obtain since some countries require it and others accept it as a valid license. In the United States, you can purchase one through the American Automobile Association (AAA), and it is valid for one calendar year.

Know what is required to drive abroad

Another part of being prepared is knowing what documents you may be required to present in order to rent a vehicle. Here are three scenarios you could run into:

1. An IDP is not required to drive in the country, just a valid passport and current driver's license issued by your native country.

2. An IDP is required, in addition to your passport and a current valid driver's license issued by your native country.

3. Not only will you need an IDP, passport, and current valid driver's license, but you will also need to obtain a special permit issued by the country you want to drive in.

As part of your pre-departure planning, you should check the requirements of the countries you want to drive in. Having the proper documents will help you avoid fines and even potential jail time.

Driving in a foreign country might not seem like something you need to prepare for, but as you've read, it absolutely is. A country's laws and unwritten rules of the road may be similar to or very different from those in your home country. You'll also want to familiarize yourself with the local road signs, as you'll more than likely pass some that you've never seen before. Distances and speed limits may also be displayed in a different unit of measurement than you're used to. And you may be forced to drive on the opposite side of the road. All of these little things added together can really stress out a driver if he or she gets behind the wheel unprepared.

Learn to be free, under the sea

Next up, learn how to swim if you don't already know how. You obviously don't need to be a pro swimmer to travel around the world, but there will likely be plenty of opportunities to jump in the water. That could mean snorkeling above the Great Barrier Reef or jumping into the clear waters of the Caribbean. Even if dipping your toes into the water is all you're interested in, you'll want to know the basics of how to swim and tread water in case of emergency. Sometimes your only transportation option will be a ferry, and like any other mode of transportation, there's never a guarantee that you'll arrive at your destination safely. Should you have to jump out unexpectedly, knowing how to tread water could end up saving your life.

SCUBA diving, on the other hand, is a skill you'll hopefully never have to know in an emergency. This is more of an activity you'll have the opportunity to participate in should you be interested. Getting SCUBA certified can be pretty expensive in Western countries (between renting gear and taking classes); so many people choose to get certified in developing countries. This certainly reduces out-of-pocket expenses, but sometimes it comes at the price of lower safety standards. Without local oversight ensuring standards, you have to hope the dive company has not taken any shortcuts to save money. If you do choose to get certified abroad, just do your research and check that your program of interest and its instructors are properly accredited.

Take an educational course

Perhaps the idea of taking a language course isn't appealing, but maybe you have some free time and want to hone another skill prior to departure. In addition to private organizations offering a variety of skills courses, consider auditing a class at your alma mater or enrolling in a night course at a local university for a semester. Think about courses that may improve your experience on the road, help you pick up freelance work, and enhance your résumé upon your return. This could include writing, photography, graphic design, computer programming, personal finance, or world politics.

 Prepare for your return before you even leave

Can you remember in detail what you did at work a year ago? If it's difficult for you to recall now, just think about how stumped you might be during a job interview when you get back from traveling. While everything is still fresh in your mind, start making a list of your soft skills, current job responsibilities, most difficult obstacles, biggest accomplishments, and any other relevant information you might want handy to review before a job interview. Consider the most common interview questions pertaining to your current job or how you handled particular situations and jot down your answers.

Besides creating an interview review sheet, take time to thoroughly update your resume and LinkedIn profile as though you're about to apply to other jobs now. Make notes for future cover letters as well. Doing this now will help you avoid writer's block later and give you less work to do upon your return. You'll be able to focus on more important things (like finding jobs to apply to and searching for housing) and you will certainly thank yourself for it!

Life skills you can master in a week
3 months prior to departure

Learn basic first aid

Did you know that anyone could sign up for and take CPR and first aid classes? They aren't restricted to particular professions or new parents. In fact, there are classes tailored for laypeople interested in getting certified. Red Cross and other organizations usually work in conjunction with businesses to offer these classes free of charge to employees, but individuals can seek them out as well. Knowledge of basic first aid is invaluable. Being able to properly treat a cut, burn, or sprain may help you avoid going to the doctor. We also encourage you go a step further and consider taking a CPR class. In addition to learning CPR, you will also learn how to levelheadedly respond to an emergency and also how to perform the Heimlich maneuver. These classes aren't free, but they also aren't expensive. Knowing how to potentially save your travel partner's or someone else's life will be worth the cost.

Know thy world and its inhabitants

Simply put, world travelers should know geography well and be able to locate more countries on a map than most people. Knowing where countries are in relation to each other will help you plan your route too. Geography is also the basis for history and politics, and being familiar with these will help you avoid making a faux pas in front of new friends on the road.

Much like learning at least a little bit of the local language, you should also learn about the culture so you can be respectful. Embarrassing yourself culturally is bound to happen, but the key is to learn from it and be cognizant of not making the same mistake twice. This applies to how you act, dress, and even eat. In many Asian countries, for example, it's considered offensive to stick chopsticks vertically into your food, as it resembles the incense sticks that people light at Buddhist temples for their dead. Taking the time to learn what are considered offensive mannerisms can prevent these awkward situations from occurring. This is why it's a good idea to start familiarizing yourselves now with the regions you and your travel partner plan to travel around.

Likewise, start breaking down the walls of what you might find to be different. Cuisine is a great place to start, as it plays an enormous role in the lives and cultures of people around the world. You don't have to be the most adventurous eater when you come across something you've never tried before, but if you expect to eat only Western food while you're abroad, you'll not only find it to be expensive, but you will also miss out on experiencing part of the local culture. Some examples are kangaroo in Australia, grasshoppers in Laos, beef brains in Italy, and blood sausage in Finland. If you are disgusted by the food that is served, just be mindful of cultural etiquette so you can act respectful to those around you, especially if you are invited to a share meal with locals.

 ### Eat everything you're comfortable with putting into your mouth

While in Penang, Malaysia, we met a Malaysian man who frequently traveled to Vietnam on business. He told us that when his associates found out he was recently married, they insisted he try certain local dishes, claiming they would be good for his virility. Sometimes they would tell him in advance what the food was and sometimes not. So he tried things like bird-infused wine and scorpions. For the most part, he was game to try whatever they put in front of him. Then they offered him a raw, recently removed snake heart, and that's where he drew the line.

It's ok to say "no" when you aren't comfortable eating something, no matter who gives it to you. Otherwise, you could easily go from being a gracious guest to the amusement of the party. During our trip, we tried to remain adventurous in what we ate, but there were certainly times when we politely declined. Remember, whether it is food or drink, at someone's home or at a restaurant, it is always okay to say "no" if you are not comfortable. You can even use the "I don't eat meat" excuse.

Your culinary experience actually begins with how you eat. If you only know how to use a fork and knife, it's time to get your hands dirty – literally! Many people, from Africa to India, eat using their hands as their utensils, but specifically their right hand (the left is considered unclean). Dishes like thali in India require you to use this right-hand-only method. If you've never seen adults eating with their hands, you might be at a loss for what the etiquette is, but you'll find that it's actually very easy to pick up. Search for videos online to understand the basics, practice at home, and then be a sly observer when you arrive in the country so you can identify nuances. Similarly, if you've never picked up chopsticks or don't consider yourself a skilled user, buy a pair and start using them instead of a fork during meals. Research the various ways people around Asia hold them (ideally watching video tutorials online), as well as best practices for using them. Nothing will better motivate you to succeed than being hungry and not being able to eat what is in front of you.

Figure out how to get around without a GPS

This begins with understanding the importance of a compass and how to use it. You don't need to go out of your way to purchase a compass, but if you already have a small one or a compass application on a smartphone you're bringing with you, you should become familiar with it since you may find it to be helpful on the road. There are a variety of unfavorable situations that could be resolved just by knowing which way north is. You may not even be embarking on a camping or trekking expedition. Maybe you're just driving through the countryside when you realize you got turned around and the roads are unmarked.

Finally, there may be times when you get lost in a city and get so turned around that you don't know which way you came from. When you know where north is, you can use that information to navigate your way back toward the subway or your hotel. This does require you getting your bearings in the first place. When you arrive in a new city, you should understand where your hotel is in relation to the airport, train or bus stations, and the sights you'll be visiting. This way, if street signs don't look familiar and there is no one around, having a map or compass with you may help you figure out your way around town.

Extend the life of your clothes

This begins with knowing how to use a needle and thread. Accidents are bound to happen. You slip and scrape open a portion of your pants, a sleeve might catch on a nail and tear, or maybe something as small as a button pops off. You may be tempted to ignore a small tear, but after a few washes and uses, the hole could become larger. You'll then have to make the decision to fix it or throw it away. Of course, buying new pants will cut into your travel budget, and you could have saved the expense had you acted sooner. Be proactive by keeping a small sewing kit in your bag (a few needles, some thread, replacement buttons, and small scissors or a pocket knife) so you or your travel partner can fix those annoying clothing issues that are unfortunately bound to happen.

If you thought your domestic skills would end with sewing, you're wrong. You'll be doing a lot of laundry on the road. Before you go, research and test out the best ways to hand-wash clothes. If you've never hand-washed clothes in a sink, bucket, or bathtub, you probably aren't aware of the various techniques. Since hand washing isn't as effective as machine-washing clothes, you need to know how to be efficient while ensuring that your clothes come out clean and without soap residue. This is important because soap residue can really irritate your skin. After you research best practices and narrow down the ones you like most, test them out at home. See how long it takes for your clothes to hang dry, too, so you have an idea of how much time you'll need whenever you decide to do laundry. If this does not seem appealing, nearly all accommodations offer laundry services, though you can expect this expense to add up quickly and take away from other things you could spend your money on. Still, hand-washing clothes is good to know in case you can't find laundry facilities, are roughing it in remote locations, or just trying to save money.

Don't pay high tourist prices

Haggling is something that can only be experienced and taught through example. Negotiating the price of socks might sound silly or like a foreign concept, but it's business-as-usual for the people of many countries. This is unfortunately something you might not be able to practice much prior to leaving, but familiarizing yourself now with how to haggle well and not get ripped off will benefit you later. As you spend more time in areas that expect you to haggle, like in Turkey, India, or Vietnam, you will learn how to be a better negotiator and not overpay.

When it comes to price negotiation, let's make an example out of a day bag. Your day bag's zipper broke and you need a new backpack. This is a time-sensitive purchase, so you can't wait too long to replace it. The bag you had was made by a popular brand and cost more than $70 at home. However, you need to divorce yourself from a Western mindset and understand that most of the products you will find in small shops (not retail outlets abroad) are black-market items and were probably acquired at a very low cost. In these instances, it will be difficult to say whether a bag's quality is low or high based on the brand name. While you might see the same exact backpack, the likelihood that it is from the same manufacturer is small. Even if it actually is, it may have been part of a defective batch that was supposed to be destroyed instead of sold. Either way, in a worst-case scenario, you buy the bag only to have break within days. This means no return policy and you're out all the money you spent. Because there is ultimately no true guarantee for you (the buyer), you want to try to pay as low of a price as possible.

The best place to start is with the price. Determine a maximum price you are willing to pay and stick to it. In this situation, let's say you come up with $15 for a new bag. (Some cities have a reputation for inflating the price of goods sold to tourists by 100% or more. Do your research and ask other travelers about their experiences to determine what a fair price is. Western prices shouldn't be paid in poorer countries either. Take all aspects of the situation into account prior to setting your max.) If you are shooting for a ceiling of $15, begin your negotiating much lower. The rule of thumb is to begin at less than half of your max. Once you begin the negotiation with your starting price, you will quickly find out whether your offer is fair or not.

When you see a bag you like, approach the vendor and ask for a closer look. You will want to examine the material, craftsmanship of the stitching, and the bag's durability. You may find vendors either let you examine it without any hassle or start pushing you to buy it right away. If they are overly aggressive and won't let you inspect the bag, then you should move on. Likewise, if it looks like shoddy workmanship (holes, jagged stitching, single stitching) or the materials (canvas, straps, zippers) are of poor quality, keep moving. However, if the bag meets your standards, ask, "How much?"

Asking the question "How much?" begins the fun dance of haggling. In most cases, if you are not on a search to buy something necessary (like a broken day bag), haggling can be a fun experience. But when you're trying to buy something you actually need, it can be frustrating, confusing, and completely draining. Usually, merchants start ridiculously high. When they do that, a few reasonable weapons in your negotiating arsenal include acting outraged, severely undercutting their offer, and starting (or pretending) to walk out. The back and forth of offers and counter offers can take a while and increase only a little bit at a time. Likely, though, by starting with a price lower than half of your max, you may be able to walk away with the item at a cost you're willing to pay. This might seem petty, but it's how vendors operate. It's give and take. They want to feel like they are making a good profit, but you have to play their game in order to pay the amount you have in mind.

 Haggling like a local

It's difficult to be a haggling newbie. There are a few things you need to know to hone your skills and ultimately get the biggest bang for your buck. Here are our tips:

1. Don't ever offer the price you want to pay and stand firm, as you'll be wasting both of your time. The vendor will try to negotiate a higher price, and you will either end up budging on your price or walking away without a new bag. One of these outcomes will happen almost every time.

2. If you can't talk the first merchant down to anywhere near your price, move on. After a few vendors reject your offer, consider whether it is actually too low or if you aren't bargaining hard enough.

3. Standing firm on a price that is too low will upset the vendor. You might not care, but it's important for these haggling merchants to do two things:
   - First, sell their products. (This is how most make their sole income.)
   - Second, save face while doing so. (In many Asian countries, for example, people do not like to show negativity or be

confrontational. If they do not like your price at all, they will be very firm about not being able to meet it. If you still push and they end up begrudgingly accepting, they'll feel upset and embarrassed.)

4. Have fun with it. Keep a positive attitude and good spirits. It may seem like a weird notion, but it's beneficial for both parties to end the transaction feeling good about it.

This negotiating game sometimes results in you walking away a loser, but other times, a winner. The key is to walk in knowing exactly what you want. Another way to be a winner is to use the sale as a bargaining chip toward something else. For example, if during your negotiations it becomes clear that you can only get the vendor down to $20 for the backpack ($5 more than your max), your travel partner should step in and say, "If we buy two of these bags, we want to pay $25." Again, you're starting a little low and will probably meet them at $30, your ideal price. Of course, this is if you are in the market for two bags (or maybe instead of a bag, your travel partner chooses a different item). Otherwise you will be spending more money unnecessarily. The goal isn't to always purchase more or spend more money, but to use that second item as a bargaining tool. Before approaching a vendor, make a plan with your travel partner, and if at any point you feel uncomfortable, walk away and regroup. Telling the merchant that you need to talk away from the shop will give you a second to get out of the pressure-cooker situation and think about whether the vendor is offering you a good deal. It may also influence him or her to come down on their price because they may think they're losing your sale.

Don't overwhelm yourself

We've given you a lot of information to consider, and your

pre-departure planning stage isn't even over yet. Don't feel overwhelmed. Like we said, these are things to consider learning before you hit the road because they can drastically improve your experience. Follow through with them when you are ready and have the time, but only if you really want to. These are supplemental skills that will enhance your travel experience, but some can also be learned on the road. But do keep this question in mind: Would you rather be learning new skills on the road or reaping the benefits of these skills while traveling?

Hindsight is always 20/20. If we had made the time, taking a language class would have been helpful, but before we knew it, that window had closed in our pre-departure schedule. Similarly, if you and/or your travel partner are interested in learning new skills, this is a good opportunity to pick them up, as a pair or an individual, before your window of opportunity closes. See what makes sense to hand off based on your partner's strengths and then work on the ones that you think you would excel at. Adding these skill-building sessions into your schedule will help add variety to your weeks as well. We know you'll later be thankful that you followed through. Good luck!

CHAPTER IN REVIEW

❑ Enroll in a course to learn another language, preferably one that you will be able to use frequently during your trip.

❑ Practice driving manual and automatic vehicles – of both the two- and four-wheeled varieties.

❑ Learn to swim and consider getting SCUBA certified.

❑ Take first aid and CPR classes.

❑ Study the geography of the regions you'll visit, then research cultural etiquette and table manners.

❑ Learn how to use a compass, basic sewing techniques, and best practices for hand-washing laundry.

❑ Practice your negotiation skills.

❑ Keep your eye on the goal and how beneficial these skills will be on the road!

CHAPTER

Actively Pursuing Your Departure
3 Months Prior to Departure

Y OU ARE THREE months away! Now that you're on track to get your home affairs in order by your departure, it's time to focus the bulk of your energy on an entirely different kind of research. The activities we'll ask you to do in this chapter will have you reading into programs, protections, and benefits that you likely have only cursorily looked at before. You may be unfamiliar with some of the research topics in this chapter, but you shouldn't shy away from any of them just because you aren't already an expert. A thorough understanding is necessary to help you make an informed decision and ensure your transition to a life of full-time travel is an easy one. So get ready to compare terms and conditions, understand the fine print in contracts, and educate yourself on everything from travel insurance to credit cards.

Purchasing health and travel insurance

Before our own RTW trip, we never bothered to explore alternate health insurance plans since the companies we each worked for offered affordable healthcare options. We compared these few plans during open enrollment each year, but beyond that we knew little about other health insurance companies and the levels of coverage they offered. The problem, of course, with employer-sponsored health insurance in America is that it's tied to your active employment. As soon as you leave the company, your health insurance is typically canceled by the end of the month.

Since quitting our jobs would leave us uninsured, we needed to research affordable plans with international coverage for our trip and potentially for our return. Both of us were in good health with no chronic problems, but we didn't want to risk traveling for more than a year without health insurance. The thought of a hospital bill draining our savings or sending us into debt was scary enough to move us to action.

Since neither of us had any serious issues that would require full coverage, we opted to research combined health and travel insurance options through reputable third-party travel agencies. (Keep in mind that while travel insurance does include some medical coverage, it's mostly geared toward emergencies and won't cover preventive services and regular doctor visits in the same way that a major provider's health insurance plan would.) If you do have a chronic or serious health issues that require you to visit a doctor regularly, you should consider researching full-coverage health plans. These will cost more but offer better protection.

The biggest obstacles we faced when researching various coverage options were identifying the coverage we thought we would need and then wading through the legalese to make sense of what was actually being offered. After looking through a few plans, we were able to make a list of the coverage points that were most important to us. If a plan did not meet our minimum requirements, we easily rejected it. Ultimately, that left us with 5 to 10 plans we liked and would need to research more.

Most companies have a side-by-side comparison chart with their plans on their website. The problem is that they all organize these charts differently, making it difficult to compare plans across companies. We found that the best solution is to make your own charts to itemize costs and the coverage points you care about most. Even though it requires a bit of extra effort, this method will organize the information that's most important to you in an easy-to-understand format.

 Nailing down coverage that's important to you

Researching insurance was a task Tara took on. She looked at the full spectrum, from full health coverage to travel insurance, and discussed our options with me during dinner most nights. Tara's focus was on health insurance, but I cared more about a plan with solid trip coverage. My first fear was that one of our bags would get lost or our camera or laptop would get stolen. Second, I worried about "act of Gods," like a volcanic eruption in Iceland that would shut down travel for weeks and cause that leg of our trip to be delayed or canceled.

These "what-if" scenarios made me push for a plan that covered cancellations, delays, and lost or stolen property. Perhaps my nonchalance about health coverage was due to our good health and feeling that we could just figure things out if we got sick on the road.

Tara's view was completely opposite: electronics and plane tickets are easy and inexpensive to replace compared to our health and the expense of a hospital bill. We didn't see eye to eye, so Tara searched for a plan that would placate us both. She narrowed it down to a handful of options and created a comparison chart that highlighted the coverage that was most important to each of us.

We ultimately agreed on one of STA Travel's combination travel-and-health-insurance plans that was underwritten by Stone Bridge Casualty Insurance Company and administered by CSA Travel Protection – both of which we researched to ensure they were reputable. If we had purchased the plan through CSA Travel Protection, we would have spent significantly more than by going through STA Travel. Additionally, we had planned to buy a tour through STA, so they bundled these two purchases together and gave us a small discount. Even though travel agencies seem like a thing of the past, they are still beneficial in the present. Working with a good travel agent may open doors to discounts you might otherwise not be able to obtain yourself.

When thinking about your own coverage, you pretty much have to predict what you may do during your trip. One level of coverage that varies among the travel-plus-health-insurance plans is based on whether you will participate in sports, activities, or extreme activities while on the road. Companies classify activities versus extreme activities differently. This is an important distinction to recognize when comparing plans since policies that cover extreme activities will be more expensive. Kayaking, for example, may be considered an activity in all of company X's plans, but in company Y's plans, kayaking is categorized as an extreme activity. If you buy company Y's plan that covers activities (not extreme activities), you can still go kayaking, of course, but if you injure yourself while doing so, they likely won't reimburse you for related bills. (These types of policies often do not have co-pays and require you to pay up front and then submit a claim to be reimbursed.)

In insurance lingo, basic plans are usually referred to as Limited coverage plans, while Comprehensive policies cover more. Some Limited plans may cover activities, but it's highly unlikely that you'll find a basic plan that covers extreme activities – you would need to pay more for a Comprehensive plan's wider coverage.

The activities that qualify as "extreme" make up quite a list, but here are some highlights for you to keep in mind: bamboo boat rafting, canoeing, canyoning, cave tubing, caving, horse trekking, hot air ballooning, micro lighting, motorcycling (up to a 125cc bike), overland expedition, river or sea kayaking, shark cage diving, and white water rafting. These activities are widely available around the world, so you'll likely have many opportunities to participate in them during your trip. You don't want to limit what you can do abroad because you wanted to save a little money. Buy the coverage that makes sense for you and will always cover you in the event of an accident. Again, be sure to read the fine print on the contracts. If you don't see an activity listed that you know you want to do, call the company and ask where it falls. You may even have to pay more for certain activities, so it's best to inquire.

If you are a professional in an athletic sport or activity, you will likely not be able to receive coverage through these types of travel plans, as most companies will not extend even Comprehensive coverage to professional athletes. Instead, you would need to talk to a representative to learn about the plans they offer that cover professionals. If you are not a professional athlete, you can simply apply for these travel plans online and don't need to call a representative unless you have specific questions or concerns you need to discuss with a live person.

Finding companies, selecting plans, and making a comparison chart

You'll want to use a few methods to find reputable insurance companies that offer international coverage. You can start with a simple search online, reading guidebooks, seeing what travel bloggers recommend, or querying social media. After gathering a few options, briefly review their plans to see if any match your coverage interests, then vet the companies that you want to move forward with. Look for scams, research how easy or difficult it is to file a claim, and read reviews to get a sense of whether these are companies you want to do business with. During this research, you will likely come across other options, and you should vet them as well.

You may end your search with as many as 10 companies that meet your base criteria, and that's fine — the more the better! Now you want to find a plan or two from each that offers the level coverage you want. But besides coverage, there are other important factors that go into selecting plans to compare. Here are some important details you will want to be aware of:

- **Cost and length of coverage**: Estimate how many months you will need coverage. What is the full cost for this time period? Are there monthly payment options?
- **Activities**: Read the fine print to learn exactly what activities or sports are covered and at what levels.
- **Existing coverage**: Look into what coverage you already have so you don't pay for something you won't need. For example, you may have a credit card that offers trip protection if you purchase tickets with the card. Or perhaps you have a health insurance policy that will remain active throughout your trip. See where the gaps are and have the health and/or travel insurance that you buy fill in those gaps.
- **Deductible**: This determines how much are you expected to

pay out of pocket before your insurance will pay a claim.

- **Discounts**: You may be able to qualify for discounts if you are a student or 25 years old or younger.
- **International coverage**: Make sure the underwriting company offers coverage in all the countries you will be visiting and that the specific plan you choose covers those destinations as well.
- **Medical evacuation coverage**: This covers the cost of transporting you to the nearest healthcare facility that is equipped to handle your injury, including bringing you to another country (this is reserved for severe cases).
- **Pre-existing conditions**: Your medical history plays an important role in determining the type of coverage offered to you. Depending on your pre-existing condition, you may qualify for fewer policies or be forced to pay an addition fee.

When you are ready to make a comparison table, list the plans horizontally across the first row and these eight criteria vertically down the first column. Fill in all of the corresponding information so it's easy to compare the benefits of each plan. Here's an example:

	Company X, Plan 1	Company X, Plan 2	Company Y, Plan 1	Company Y, Plan 2
Cost				
Activities				
Existing coverage				
Deductible				
Discounts				
International coverage				
Medical evac. coverage				
Pre-existing conditions				

Depending on the plan you choose, the insurance company may not let you move forward until they decide whether they want to insure you. Some plans just let you enter your credit card information and insure you, but others tie your health directly to the plan. One thing you may have to do to qualify is get a physical examination and submit your results. The rationale is that if you are in poor health, you are a risk that the company would prefer not to take on – or maybe charge more to cover. This is rather unfortunate since pre-existing conditions such as a disease, chronic illness, or even a pregnancy may disqualify you from certain plans or saddle you with a higher premium. If you think you have a pre-existing condition, just keep this in mind while researching to help you find a plan that is right for you.

Check into possible discounts to help maximize your money on a health insurance plan. One way to cut the cost of your plan is to purchase it through a third party like a travel agency, as they typically are able to offer plans at a lower rate than if you went through the insurance company directly. Additionally, you and your travel partner may be able to save even more if you purchase your plans together, as couples' (and family) plans may be priced lower per person than individual coverage. Finally, take advantage of all student or youth discounts if you're able to. They are plentiful for those who are 25 and younger, though the student-only discounts will likely require proof of enrollment, like a student ID.

Now we'll skip ahead and assume that you have done the research and found a perfect plan. The policy fits your budget, the destinations you may be visiting, and the activities you hope to do. The last thing you'll have to determine is when to activate and terminate your coverage. If you live in a country with socialized medicine, then getting health insurance that predates your departure and extends beyond your expected return date is unnecessary. However, those who live in countries without socialized medicine may decide to use travel-health insurance as a stopgap between the day their employer-sponsored health insurance ends and when they return and purchase a dedicated domestic plan or find employment that offers insurance. It should be noted that most travel-health insurance plans do cover you in your home country, but with the caveat that you are not within a certain distance of your permanent home address. This enables you to receive treatment if you are traveling domestically, but also not use the policy as a complete health insurance replacement. Because of this distance restriction, you should try to make your last day of employment as close to your departure date as possible – unless you plan to leave town right after your current health insurance plan ends. Otherwise, if you have an insurance gap and need to see a doctor, the out-of-pocket cost might wreak havoc on your savings and trip plans. Keep these issues in mind when determining the start and end dates of your coverage.

Health insurance is important to have on an international trip, but what about travel insurance? Travel or trip insurance is often overlooked by travelers who assume that the airline, bus, or train company will protect them from in the event of a delay or cancellation. While some companies may offer food or airfare vouchers for cancellations, they don't all operate by the same standards. When you have travel insurance, you can submit a claim to be reimbursed by your insurance company, albeit some time after the fact. Beyond covering you in the case of a transportation delay or cancellation, travel insurance can also reimburse you for purchases made as a result of lost luggage or delays – just be sure to keep all receipts. Some policies also offer theft protection (up to a certain value), which can give you peace of mind if you plan to bring expensive electronics like a smartphone, laptop, or digital camera.

Choosing travel insurance that best fits your needs

We've talked a lot about health insurance and what to think about when selecting a plan. Now, using the same comparison chart that you did in the last exercise, list the following items vertically and your top travel policies horizontally. Compare the plans and determine which works best for your wants and needs.

- **Cost and length of coverage**: Estimate how many months you will need coverage. What is the full cost for this time period? Are there monthly payment options?
- **Delay and cancellation reimbursement**: This applies to natural disasters, bad weather, and even poor health – yours or your travel companion's –that might cause a delay or cancellation of your whole trip or part of it. When something like this happens, you can file a claim to receive partial or complete reimbursement for transportation you have already purchased.
- **Credit card coverage**: Some credit cards offer travel insurance benefits, such as delayed or lost luggage, insurance for car rentals, and emergency assistance insurance. You don't want to pay extra for such coverage in your travel insurance if you are already covered by a credit card you plan to use.
- **Homeowner's insurance**: If you have homeowner's insurance and intend to keep it during your trip, you may find that you are covered for certain lost or stolen items.
- **Refund policy**: Some policies will refund the full cost of reservations in the event you need to cancel or delay your trip. However, this is done on a weighted scale, so the further in advance you notify your insurance company, the more money you are likely to recoup (in other words, you may receive a 100% reimbursement if you cancel months in advance, but nothing if you try to cancel the day before).
- **Repatriation of remains**: While this may not be something you would ever want to think about, this important part of travel

insurance will help cover the repatriation of your or your travel partner's remains to your home country in the event that the unthinkable happens.

There is certainly a lot to look into and think about when it comes to travel and health insurance. All of the research and effort may even leave you wondering if you can just throw chance to the wind and travel without it. Maybe you're young and in good health, and perhaps this seems like an unnecessary expense for you since minor injuries and illnesses may not justify the cost. Yes, that may very well be true, but there are two things you need to consider before declining coverage. First, accidents happen regardless of age and health. The second reason isn't so obvious. Most organized tours require you to have proof of travel insurance. This usually does not apply to single-day tours, but most multi-day tours do, especially if the tour is run through an international agency. You never know what opportunities you might have on the road, and while you may not plan to sign up for a tour prior to departure, not having the proper insurance may prevent you from joining one later.

From our own experience, out of our 14 months of continuous travel, we did not utilize our health or travel insurance once. There were definitely times when we could have (illness and lost luggage were reasons), but the claims process seemed like more effort than it was worth for the return we'd potentially get (out-of-pocket costs were minor for us in these instances). Despite this, our insurance did have two main benefits. The most important to us was the peace of mind it provided. If an emergency did occur, we had coverage. Also, without insurance, we wouldn't have been able to join three multi-week tours during our travels. We're not really "tour people," as we much prefer to explore destinations at our own pace, but some actually saved us money and others provided an educational experience we wouldn't have been able to get through independent travel.

Finding a bank for your international lifestyle

Now that you're practically an expert in insurance policies and fine print, it is time to shift gears and look into banking institutions, credit cards, and debit cards. Let's start with banks. While your current banking institution may be a good fit for your life now, it may turn out to be less than satisfactory while traveling abroad. It comes down to incentives. Many banks will offer a high interest rate or no monthly fees if you maintain a certain balance or utilize direct deposit through work. But once you hit the road, you may no longer be depositing money and will only be withdrawing, which will likely at some point bring your remaining funds below the required minimum balance. Suddenly, you might be faced with monthly fees, service charges, or other maintenance deductions from your account. To avoid this, you definitely want to be proactive and talk to a representative from your bank about certain scenarios and what requirements or potential charges may be associated with your account.

The goal of this task is to find an account that will best suit your future international lifestyle, and you may find yourself switching banking institutions to do so. There are a few important factors to consider when comparing accounts:

1. Are there monthly service fees? There are so many banks these days that are fee-free that it's not worth your time to bother with any that charge maintenance or below-minimum-balance fees.

2. Do they charge for money transfers? Maybe you decide to open a couple accounts with one institution (like your No-Touch Account and World Travel Fund). You may run into a situation where you need to transfer money between those accounts or between your World Travel Fund and an account at another bank. Transfer fees, like monthly service fees, are really a thing of the past, and so you don't want to do business with a bank that will charge you for it.

3. Is there a debit card replacement fee? If you lose your debit card and you don't have a backup, you may not be able to withdraw money from an ATM without incurring a hefty fee (like if you were to use a credit card at an ATM for what's called a cash advance). Some banks also charge for expedited delivery of your new card.

4. How helpful is their customer service department? This is extremely important. Looking back at our checking account mishap in Iceland in chapter 1, if our bank's customer service hadn't taken responsibility and hadn't been so helpful, we would have lost out on more than $100 USD. It's important that your money is in the hands of an institution that you trust and will be there for you when an emergency happens.

There is enough competition in the market that you will likely be able to find one bank that satisfies all your requirements. Often, you can even see if they can sweeten the pot by adding a benefit that another bank advertises, even if it's for a short-lived promotional period. It certainly never hurts to ask! After we researched banks, we ultimately settled on one* that provided us with all the features we were looking for, in addition to no ATM fees worldwide (at the end of the month, they reimburse to your account any fees that were incurred) and no foreign transaction fees for purchases made with our debit card (other institutions charge anywhere from 1 to 3% of the transaction price). These two perks easily saved us hundreds of dollars over the course of our trip.

*****Note from the authors:** We chose not to reveal the name of the banking institution and credit cards we used during our trip since the market is dynamic and options are constantly changing. Additionally, since everyone has different preferences, the companies we chose to do business with may not be the best option for you and your needs.

Selecting credit cards that are right for you

In many global locations, your credit card will be your most efficient means of payment (though there are definitely cities and countries where cash is king). When you do have the option to use your credit card, there are a few reasons it is better to err on the side of paying with it versus cash. First, it's never wise to carry large amount of cash, as it will make you a target for thieves and also cause you to worry about being targeted. If your credit card is lost or stolen, the company that issued the card will work on your behalf to cancel and replace the card and ensure that any fraudulent charges not be your responsibility. Also, you lose money each time you exchange one currency for another. So if you take out too much cash in any one country and need to exchange it to another currency before leaving, you're paying two transaction fees instead of one. Any opportunity to minimize conversions will save you money.

A good credit score is the first step to getting the credit card you want. If you are American, you can simply request a copy of your credit report online, which is a free service once a year (any more requests during the same calendar year will be subject to a fee). If you have a history of making payments on time, from small ongoing debts like a cell phone bill or student loans to larger ones like a mortgage, you will likely have a solid credit score. A score of 720 or higher is generally considered good, though standards for what is a "good" or "excellent" score do differ among lenders. Generally, the higher your score, the less of a risk you are for the lender, qualifying you for premium cards, a higher credit limit, and a better interest rate.

Now it is time to figure out which card suits you best. You'll find that each has a unique value proposition since the competition is so fierce among credit card companies vying to make you their cardholder. Some may waive the annual fee for the first year, others offer a gratis concierge service, and some cards come with a microchip. While a card with additional services or those marketed as a "traveler card" may sound attractive, don't let it distract you from the core features you'll need for your trip. A perfect card for travelers will ultimately save them money and offer reliable fraud and purchase protection.

Credit cards can save you money in a variety of ways. First, you should definitely look for a card that does not charge a foreign transaction fee. Many don't nowadays, so there's no point in paying the fee when you can use a card that waives it. Second, most cards offer car rental insurance and trip cancellation and trip interruption insurance. So if you use your card to pay for a car rental, you can decline the insurance offered through the rental agency. And if the card does offer trip insurance, you can utilize those benefits if you pay for an aspect of your trip with your card, say a flight, and the flight is delayed or canceled.

Third, research how you would be awarded points based on purchases. You'll be spending money every day during your trip, so it will be an easy opportunity to rack up points that can be applied back toward your trip. Look for a card that offers a high amount of points for every dollar spent, and review their reward program to see what you can apply your points toward. Will their cash-back option maximize your points, or would they be better spent toward airfare or hotel stays through a different card?

Also, you'll want to apply for a card that offers a large amount of bonus points upon signup and additional points if you spend a certain amount of money within the first few months of opening the card. If you're worried about hitting the target amount, just wait until you have the card to buy big-ticket items for your trip – like gear, tours, and plane tickets – to ensure you spend the minimum amount to qualify for the bonus points. Some cards will issue additional bonus points if you add another cardholder to your account, like your spouse (ask a representative about this if you don't see the offer mentioned online). These are free, easy points to obtain, and depending on the type of card, you may be able to apply the points toward hotel reservations, plane tickets, and other travel-related expenses.

Finally, examine the services, inclusions, and discounts you'll have access to with the card. For example, airline-sponsored cards may offer a free checked bag and access to airport lounges. Other cards may have partner companies that offer a fixed discount with every purchase. And don't underestimate the value of the concierge service. If you haven't had time to look for a hotel in Paris that fits your budget, just call them up and the concierge on duty will do the research for you. This is a valuable service to take advantage of during your pre-departure planning as well.

Most of the best cards with the best perks charge an annual fee. This isn't necessarily a bad thing, but you'll want to make sure the benefits they offer are worth the fee and that you'll actually take advantage of these perks. Ask that the fee be waived for the first year as you "test out the card." If the fee is under $100, many representatives will waive it for you to entice you to sign up. If you do get the fee waived, you could essentially take full advantage of the card for up to one year and then cancel it before the end of your first 12 months to avoid paying the fee for the second year. Even if you aren't able to get the fee waived for the first year, you may find that the bonus points offered upon signup offset the annual fee.

Things to know about credit card reward programs

Depending on your credit card program, your rewards may be offered as points, miles, or cash back. It is easy to assume these are equal, but unfortunately they are not point-for-point or dollar-for-dollar across cards. You'll want to do some comparative research to see which card will maximize your money and your rewards. These are a few additional concepts to consider as well:

- **Anniversary bonus**: This is a yearly bonus (5,000 points, for example) that may cancel out the annual fee.
- **Category incentives**: Some programs offer more rewards for certain types of purchases. For example, instead of earning 1 point per dollar, you may earn 1.5 points for every dollar spent on restaurant purchases and 2 points for every dollar spent on gas.
- **Off-peak travel**: If you want to trade in your points or miles for a flight or vacation package, some programs actually reward you for traveling during low season by offering a higher return for your points or miles.
- **Availability**: Even though you have enough points or miles, the airline you want to book with may not have availability for the dates you want travel. Be sure that the rewards program offers multiple options and not just a couple.
- **Blackout dates**: These are specific dates when you aren't allowed to trade in your points or miles for travel rewards, though some cards don't have any blackout dates. If there are blackout dates, they are typically during holidays and high travel seasons.
- **Extra charges**: Check to see if your program adds a fuel surcharge, booking fee, or service charge in addition to trading in your points. Some may even charge ad additional fee for one-way tickets, stopovers, and checked baggage.

- **Phone service fee**: If you're on the road and don't trust the Internet connection, you may need to call to book a reward ticket or hotel stay. Often, there is a convenience fee associated with this service.
- **Transferability**: If you want to transfer your rewards to partner programs (airlines, hotels, car rental agencies), find out if the transfer takes long. Some programs may take up to a week to transfer points while others do it instantly.
- **Transfer bonuses**: Transferring large amounts of points to a partner can result in bonuses, meaning your 20,000 points may increase to 25,000 points just because you made the transfer.
- **Gifting**: You may decide to send miles or points to a friend, relative, or charity (some charities accept miles in lieu of monetary donations). Find out if this service is free or charge or if transferring them to someone else's account will cost you.
- **Service fees**: Beware of those that charge a service fee to redeem points for products or cash back. And if you're making a booking yourself, there shouldn't be a fee associated with that either.

Personally, we were able to find one card that met all the requirements we had in mind, though it lacked a microchip, which is a security measure designed to cut down on fraud. The technology is considered more secure because it is difficult to counterfeit these types of cards. Tighter security wasn't the reason we wanted a card with a microchip, though. While microchips were not popular in America at the time, we thought we would need a card with a chip in certain countries we were planning to visit. We didn't want to be in a situation where our card wouldn't be accepted and we therefore couldn't pay for goods or services. So we ultimately got two credit cards for our trip. One was our primary card that had all the benefits we wanted and the other was a secondary card that had the microchip in it (for use only when absolutely needed). Europe ended up being the only region where we used the technology.

Likewise, we recommend that you also carry at least two different cards in case one is declined, lost, or stolen.

Start looking into credit cards at least three months prior to your departure. This will allow you to become comfortable with the card's reward program, the method for point redemption, and how to navigate the online account system. Plus, you'll be able to begin accruing points sooner than later. You also don't want to be in a situation where you're a week away from departure and you're still waiting for your card to be mailed. Be prepared to wait up to a couple weeks to receive your card and longer before your bonus points are added to your account (this may take up to 12 weeks). Once you have your new card in hand, set up auto-pay by linking it to your World Travel Fund account. By having your balance automatically deducted from your bank account every month, you won't have to ever worry about making payments on the road. This will help you avoid late fees or being charged penalty interest for not paying in full.

Don't forget to pack your passport

Two important question here: do you plan to travel internationally, and if so, do you have a passport already? If you don't have a passport, you should apply for one sooner than later, as they can be time-consuming to obtain. Americans are able to apply at most post offices, so it wouldn't be necessary to travel to New York or Washington, D.C. to get one, unless you want it expedited or want an excuse to travel there. However, if you already have a passport, great! But check the expiration date. Will it still be valid for at least six months by the end of your travels? Some countries require that foreign visitors carry passports that have at least 6 months validity remaining upon entry. Rules and regulations differ by country, but this requirement may prohibit you from entering a country you want to visit.

Which passport will I stamp today?

Those who have dual citizenship can travel with two passports, and thus have quite an advantage over those with single-country citizenship. These dual citizens could have acquired another citizenship by birth (some countries extend citizenship to those physically born there) while others will grant citizenship through marriage, based on a parent's nationality (even if a child was not born in that country), or through sponsorship and naturalization. The latter example requires a person to live in a country for a certain period of time that culminates with courses and an examination about the country. Depending on the country and your home country, you may be able to obtain dual citizenship or you may be required to renounce your original citizenship.

Now back to the advantage that dual citizenship offers. These travelers can use whichever passport they want when entering a country, though they must be sure to use the same one when exiting. The benefit is that they may pay less for a visa or may not need to obtain a visa at all if they use a certain passport (since visa requirements differ among countries). They may also find that they are easily granted entry with one nationality but not with the other. If you are a dual citizen, you should definitely consider the benefits and drawbacks of taking both passports with you on your trip.

Equally as important as your passport's validity is the number of empty stamp pages it holds. You will unavoidably use more pages than you expect during long-term travel. It's actually amazing how quickly the pages fill as careless immigration officers stamp in the middle of a page, causing it to be too filled for others to stamp on since some countries require an unmarked page or half a page for entry (there are pages in our passports that contain five stamps and others that received, and will now only receive, one stamp). U.S.

citizens applying for a new passport will automatically receive 17 pages available for visas and stamps, but 26 additional pages can also be inserted free of charge – just be sure to check the request box on your application! We had to get more pages added on the road, in Cambodia, and it cost each of us $82. A costly lesson indeed.

Visa is not just a type of credit card

As you travel, your passport will likely put you in one of two categories. There's the category where travel is relatively easy and inexpensive. Then there is the category where entry into countries difficult and pricey. Where you fall will be the result of how your country fits into the global "playground." If your country "plays" well with others, you may find visas to be inexpensive, available upon arrival instead of in advance, or not even required. Even so, many abide by reciprocity and may charge you a hefty price for a visa because your homeland charges their citizens the same fee. Back when we advised you to start planning a tentative route, we recommended that you look into whether you can even enter countries you were interested in visiting. That was where we stopped, and cost and the ease of getting a visa took a backseat to whether it was even possible to attain one. But now that you are three months from departing, it is time to revisit your route from a visa perspective.

In most cases, you will be applying for a tourist visa. These are by far the easiest type to obtain (student, business, and volunteer/employment visas sometimes require sponsorship paperwork from schools, companies, individuals, or other organizations), and each country should maintain an official government website dedicated to the requirements and costs of their visas. When you apply for a visa, you can visit a country's embassy or consulate in person if you live near it. They will either immediately affix a visa to an empty page or you may have to leave your passport at the office for up to a few weeks while they review your paperwork. Living in or by a major city that has embassies or consulates will definitely save you time and money, but if you don't, you will need to work with a visa service or travel agency or mail in your passport and documents yourself. We urge travelers to obtain visas in advance whenever possible, though be cognizant of each visa's validity period, as visas do expire a fixed amount of time after their date of issue (typically three months).

 ## Maddeningly close to visas we could not get

Prior to our departure we were residents of Washington, D.C. This presented us with the favorable situation of living within miles of embassies and consulates of the countries we anticipated visiting during the trip. Being able to make a lunch-hour appointment to apply for a visa would have been much easier than figuring out how to get the same visa in another country during the trip. However, as we mentioned previously, visas have a validity period, and most are for 3 months after the issue date. Therefore, most of visas we needed would no longer be valid by the time we arrived in the country. Some countries offered the ability to get a 5-year visa, for example, but we had to ask ourselves whether the extra cost was worth the ease (it wasn't) and if we honestly thought we would visit the country again years later (we didn't feel the need after the first visit). We ended up not applying for those extended visas at home, and we're actually glad we didn't because it wasn't too difficult to obtain any visa on the road. Sometimes we had to stay in one city longer than we anticipated to ensure we had time to get a visa, and sometimes we went out of our way to certain cities with embassies that are known for making the process quick and easy. While this may seem like more of a hassle than obtaining visas in your hometown (and don't get us wrong, because it is), it's still part of the adventure of traveling.

Being strategic about which visas you get before leaving, and therefore which countries you visit first, can save you a lot of time and reduce stress on the road since some visas can take weeks to obtain. For example, we chose to make Russia our third stop, and so were able to get the visa prior to departure. Even though we dropped off our applications in person, it still took more than two weeks for the Russian consulate to return our passports with visas inside. Can you imagine applying for a visa in another country and having to wait two weeks to get your passport back? Without your passport in a foreign country, you cannot rent a car, hop a flight, or check into a hotel (depending on the manager, you may be able to get around this last one) since foreigners typically have to present their passport upon check-in. You basically have to wait in the one city until your passport is available for pickup. So if a country is known for a long visa turnaround time, you'll certainly want to get it at home if you can.

As we've previously mentioned, if you are traveling for more than three months, you will most likely apply for a few visas on the road. A few countries offer e-visas, which can be obtained online, but most countries require you to obtain one upon arrival or at a consulate prior to entering the country, which isn't always a simple process. This is mostly because not every consulate offers visa-issuing services and the consulates that do are not in each capital or major city around the world.

Therefore, you need to plan ahead by knowing which visas you need, where you can obtain them, and the site's processing hours and holiday closure schedule. When applying for visas on the road, you should be prepared with all required documentation, such as extra passport-sized photos; proof of onward travel (an outbound flight from the visa-issuing country); proof of adequate funds (a bank statement to show you can buy a ticket out of the country); sponsorship from a school, employer, or tour agency, if necessary;

and your vaccination card (to prove you received a yellow fever vaccination where required, for example).

You will need to prove you got shot up

Your health card (a yellow card that tracks your immunizations) is just as important as your passport is for gaining entry into some countries. So it goes without saying that you should be thinking of which travel vaccinations you will need to get before you leave. We encourage you to start thinking about vaccinations now (and perhaps even making an appointment at a travel vaccination clinic) since some require a series of shots and take several weeks to administer (for example, rabies and Japanese encephalitis). Many insurance plans cover the majority of travel vaccinations, but even if yours doesn't and you need to pay out of pocket, consider the potential consequences should you decide not to get vaccinated. Is it worth the risk of having to treat an illness on the road, or contracting one that may be with you for life?

If your health insurance doesn't cover travel vaccinations and the cost to you is incredibly expensive, you may be able to get your vaccinations on the road for a fraction of the cost. For example, the Red Cross in Bangkok offers inexpensive immunizations. We researched this option but ultimately got all of our vaccinations at home since Asia was the last region we visited during our trip. However, the process does seem easy and fairly transparent for foreign travelers based on the experiences we read about.

Beyond vaccinations, you'll want to stock up on any medication that you need to take or will need to take on a regular basis. You can certainly purchase the same or a similar medication on the road, and sometimes at a lower cost, though you should be cognizant of the strength of the pills the pharmacy dispenses versus what you are currently prescribed. You'll also want to be aware of pharmacies that may sell counterfeit medication, which could contain additives or may not be as potent or effective.

There are certainly a lot of tasks and research we've recommended in this chapter, and you should strive to do as many as possible before you leave. The decisions you make for these topics will have a large impact throughout your trip. Since some of these steps may take weeks or months to complete, it is best to start immediately so you have enough time and don't feel rushed. We do feel as though three months will be enough to complete them, but should you need more time, you may want to consider pushing your departure date back so you aren't scrambling or stressed out on the road.

CHAPTER IN REVIEW

❑ Compare insurance plans to find one that suits both your needs and budget.

❑ Health and travel insurance are required by some tours, so even if you plan not to purchase it, you may have to sign up for a basic plan.

❑ Find a credit card that will maximize your money and your reward points. Pay especially close attention to foreign transaction and service fees.

❑ Make sure your passport will have at least 6 months' validity by the end of your trip and that you have all the appropriate visas in advance of arrival in any given country.

❑ Make an appointment at a travel vaccination clinic to ensure you receive all the shots you will need prior to departure.

❑ Don't forget that some vaccinations are required in order to enter a country, as well as proof that you received them.

CHAPTER 8

Supplies to Pack That Don't Plug In
3 Months Prior to Departure

NOW THAT YOU'RE getting closer to your departure date, it should feel like everything is really starting to come together for your trip. By now, you have been saving, downsizing, researching, and narrowing down the faraway places you might visit. While the tasks we recommended in previous chapters have generally required you to make hard choices and probably weren't too much fun, this chapter is will guide you through a tangible, and therefore more exciting, part of your trip – your luggage and what you should pack!

Between this chapter and the next, where we dive into which electronics to bring, you not only have the ultimate packing list for long-term travel, but also guidance on how to think strategically about each item. By being clever and thorough now, you will save time and money on the road!

Find and buy a bag you will love

Most people have a preference for one of three categories of luggage: a bag with wheels, an oversized backpack, or an oversized backpack with wheels. This is one of the age-old debates among travelers, and there are valid reasons for all types. For long-term travel, however, our preference is to carry an oversized backpack and not a wheeled bag. These bags are designed to rest on your hips so you aren't carrying the weight with your back or shoulders, whereas other types of luggage rely on wheels and arm strength.

While you should certainly move forward with the bag you prefer, we want to give you the main reasons why we recommend large backpacks for a long-term trip. First, when luggage handlers at airports or bus stations toss bags around, wheeled luggage are more susceptible to damage, like breaking a wheel or cracking the handle. Bags with wheels are also more difficult to manage when you are walking on gravel, uneven pavement, up stairs, or running to catch a bus. Our experiences have proved time and again that oversized backpacks last longer, allow you to be more mobile, and are lighter (since they lack wheels and the retractable handle mechanism). Since our recommendation is to purchase an oversized backpack and not a wheeled bag, we'll be focusing this section on these "backpacker bags."

If you currently own a pack and have had it for a while, thoroughly examine it to decide whether it can last a long journey with daily use and abuse. Depending on where you travel and how you travel, your pack could encounter dirt, grease, rough handling, and bottom-of-the-pile treatment. These types of bags aren't easy to replace while traveling since they are mostly sold in specialty stores.

For those purchasing their first backpacker bag, it's best to go to a store that specializes in outdoor gear. Knowledgeable and experienced employees will be able to walk you through the different styles, how they should fit and feel, and ultimately which options will be best for your trip. You don't necessarily have to buy the bag at the store – you can purchase it online if the price is lower – but it's worthwhile to test a few out in-person to get the right one for you.

Buying a bag that does not fit you properly can result in severe injuries. To avoid hurting yourself, there are a couple points you need to remember when finding the right bag. First, the bag should rest on your hips and snuggly grip your waist with a resizable belt. There are actually higher-end bags that offer heat-moldable belts that are literally baked specifically to your form and size. However, most bags accommodate a range of hip sizes with belts that you can tighten and loosen (which are likely the better option for long-term travel since you may lose or gain weight during your trip). Second, the height of the bag should be sized to match your torso. Remember that your belt size refers to your waist while your torso length is a measurement from the most noticeable protrusion on your upper spine to the lower protrusion of your hips. This is currently measured in inches and, much like shoe shopping, you should come prepared with this information before trying on bags.

Once you have your measurements, you'll want to think about which size bag is right for you. They range from small daypacks that hold 20 liters to extended-travel packs that can hold upwards of 80 liters. (Backpacks around the world are measured by volume capacity in liters.) Be sure to test out various size options at the store by filling a bag with other items, strapping it on, and walking around for a few minutes. Yes, a few minutes with each, not just up and down an aisle once, so that you can get a good feel for how the bag sits and if it's too large or too small.

As you test products, remember that this purchase isn't one to skimp on. By all means, buy a pack that is on sale (they are expensive), but do avoid getting an off-brand or knock-off product to save a little money. Your bag will be the closest thing you will have to a safe or storage unit during your trip. It will hold your possessions, and a broken zipper on your main compartment is equivalent to a house with a kicked-in front door. Try to find a pack made from canvas or a heavy-duty material. Any zippers and buckles should look large and robust. Test them out and tug at them to make sure they're secure and durable.

Another thing to keep in mind is that you do not want to purchase a bag with too many loose outside straps that you cannot easily tuck away. Outside straps are more beneficial to hikers and campers, not travelers. Loose straps are notorious for getting stuck in airport conveyor belts, and some airlines may not let you fly with straps sticking out. Duct tape could come in handy in this instance, but you might as well buy a hassle-free bag to begin with.

Speaking of hassle-free, try to avoid buying a top-loading pack. That is, of course, unless you would enjoy a scavenger hunt whenever you need something that isn't right on top. This style makes it very difficult to access items that are in the middle or, worse, on the bottom. If you do manage to pull your hoodie from the bottom of your bag, you probably will inadvertently drag out several items with it, making for a messy pack that you have to reorganize often. Better-designed bags offer multiple entry points, making it easier to access items stored in various parts of the pack. As a bonus, some are sold with detachable day bags, which typically zip onto the outside of the larger back. They are handy add-ons that you can either keep attached to the outside of your pack or use as a counterweight to wear in front of you (also allowing you to have a closer eye on your most valuable items).

What bag do you want on your back?

There are myriad backpacker-friendly bags on the market. Finding the "right" one is a matter of personal preference. Here are some questions to think about when trying to decide which backpack might be right for you:

- Make sure it fits you comfortably. There is a reason there are men's and women's backpacks. The height should be just right and the weight should be distributed on your hips, not your shoulders and back. These features should be adjustable too.
- How secure is it? Can all zipper pulls lock together? Are there hidden compartments to store valuables?
- How do you access the contents of the bag? Are there multiple entry points? (Save yourself headaches by avoiding top-loading bags!)
- Are the straps and backside padded? Does it offer ventilation along your spine? If not, it'll be a miserable journey!
- Is it expandable? You may decide to buy souvenirs or new clothes. Can the bag create extra room without you having to ditch stuff?
- Is its material waterproof or does it come with a rain cover?
- Does it have room for a hydration pack or water bottle? Look for storage internally or a loop or mesh netting on the outside to easily clip on or access a bottle.
- Is this model known to wear quickly or last long? Read reviews to find out before you buy.
- Always test your favorites in the store by packing weight of any kind then walking around the store for a few minutes to see how you feel. After you buy one, test it out again. Just because you had a good experience with a pack in a store does not mean it will feel good loaded with your actual gear. When you get home, load it up with heavy items and walk around the block a few times (at least 10 minutes to simulate walking from a bus station

to your hostel). Don't worry about looking silly; it's better to find out right away whether the pack feels comfortable than to wait until you've hit the road. If it's not comfortable, return it and try another one.

A rain cover is a crucial part of your bag that will not only keep your belongings inside the bag dry but it also helps protect your pack from dirty, dusty, and grimy conditions. A cover offers the subtle fringe benefit of deterring thieves looking for a quick grab. Most thieves look for easy targets, and covering your pack creates an obstacle by hiding your zippers and compartments. Anyone looking to rob you would have to steal the whole unwieldy bag or slash it with a blade to get to its internal contents. Minimizing the risk of theft will dramatically decrease the chances you will be robbed while walking or transporting your bag. Personally, we found that staying vigilant about using our rain covers even when it wasn't raining helped us walk away from a 14-month trip with nothing stolen out of our packs. We like to think that using our respective rain covers during transportation days made our bags seem less accessible than uncovered bags.

Many backpacks come with a rain cover, but if the one you're eyeing doesn't, you can always purchase a cover separately. There are downsides to buying a rain cover separately, though. It is an additional expense (and not cheap) and likely won't be a perfect fit for your bag. For example, you may want a 70-liter bag, but perhaps the only rain covers available are 65 and 75 liters. Also, the rain covers that are included with bags are most likely manufactured to fit the entire bag perfectly, whereas those sold separately try the one-size-fits-all approach and may not protect the entire bag completely. The difference in how the two fit is like putting on a ski mask (those that come with the bag) versus a hairnet (those sold separately).

How to slash-proof your bag

Backpack protections like hidden compartments and using a rain cover may deter thieves from targeting your bag, but you should also consider a DIY solution that has the added benefit of increasing your bag's durability. In some high-theft cities, criminals have been known to use a blade to slash the bottom or front of travelers' packs. Since backpacks are usually stuffed to maximum capacity, any possessions around the cut will easily fall out. Working alone or with another crook, they grab whatever possessions hang out or fall to the ground. It could happen while you are preoccupied with finding the right street to turn on, and you may not even know that a theft occurred. If you do notice, you may not be able to do anything about it since you will be encumbered with the bag. It is a quick and dirty robbery.

While this type of theft isn't popular and certainly not one you should fear while traveling, you should still be proactive and protect yourself as much as possible. Here are instructions for how to slash-proof your bag, which will even protect the contents of your bag from inadvertent tears or cuts that may happen while traveling.

What you need:
- ❏ 3-4 lightweight plastic cutting boards (they should be thick but flexible enough to bend easily)
- ❏ scissors
- ❏ hole punch
- ❏ heavy-duty needle
- ❏ heavyweight thread

How to do it:
1. Measure the bottom base of your bag. Then unzip each flap and measure the inside width and height. You don't need to measure the sides or the part that lies flush with your back.

2. You'll want to use two cutting boards for each area of your bag for stronger protection. If the boards are too large, trim them with scissors to fit each area.

3. Punch holes near the edges of the cutting boards, which will help you sew them onto your bag (instead of punching the needle through the board material). Note: The double boards that will sit on the bottom of your bag do not need to be sewn in since they likely won't fall through a single cut. Of course, you should do it if you think it would help protect the contents of your bag better.

4. Using a needle and thread, sew the boards onto your bag.

We took those steps to slash-proof our bags, and while we never encountered a blade-wielding thief, we felt peace of mind that our bags were protected, which goes a long way when you're traveling and already outside of your comfort zone.

Juggling practicality, fashion, and comfort

Now that you have your pack squared away, it's time to start filling it! Packing for four seasons and the extremes of each of them can lead you to quickly overfill your bag, not to mention the weight you'd have to carry. If you already have an itinerary in mind, then choosing clothes for your trip is a little easier. However, if you aren't sure where you'll be after your third month, pack for your first few destinations. For example, if you are starting in Saint Petersburg, Russia, you'll want to pack some warm items. If the rest of your trip ends up taking you to tropical beaches, you can easily buy a bathing suit and shorts on the road, and vice versa.

But before you even start thinking about your shirts-to-pants ratio or how many long-sleeved shirts to pack, let's start with the basics.

There are three main considerations that tie into creating your travel wardrobe: color, multi-purpose items, and drying time. The one characteristic they all must have is utility, and we'll explain why. Let's start with the first.

Even though you may not think that the colors you choose to pack have a purpose, they do and should. Take dark-hued clothes for example. They hide stains and wrinkles well, which are two unavoidable things that all backpackers will encounter. Dark and neutral colors are also beneficial if you plan to go on safari. Animals tend to differentiate bright colors easier than khaki or dark clothes, which blend in better with nature. On the flip side, if you plan to run outdoors, you should wear bright colors as you would at home. This will help drivers spot you more easily when you're crossing the street.

Another consideration is to make sure the items you pack have multiple purposes. You don't have to find shorts that double as a vest, but the shorts you bring should serves more than one or two purposes. It might be difficult for you to look at a pair of shorts and come up with more than one way to use them, but once you consider the various scenarios for when you would wear shorts, you'll realize that you cannot pack a pair for every single occasion. For example, you would want one or two versatile pairs that could be used for sleeping, hiking, sightseeing, relaxing at a cafe, going to the beach, and jogging or exercising.

A wide scarf is a great example of an inexpensive, multipurpose travel must-have. While a bandana will do in a pinch, the size of a scarf is what makes it so versatile. In cold weather, you can wrap it around your neck, drape it over your shoulders, or use it like a blanket to keep you warm. When it's warm outside, you can use it to wipe away sweat or wrap it like a sarong around your waist or around your head to help protect against the sun (like camel riders in the desert!). Speaking of deserts, if you're in the Sahara and a sandstorm is approaching, you can use it to cover your eyes and mouth (this helped us numerous times). It can also double as a sling, tourniquet, or bandage (albeit a temporary non-sterile one). When you're on transportation and want to nap, you can bundle it up to serves as a soft makeshift pillow. For female travelers, a scarf can double as a head or shoulder covering, which will be essential when visiting certain religious sites and when walking around conservative countries. The other great thing about scarves is their availability. If you lose yours or don't bring one when you leave home, you can easily find them in a variety of styles and materials practically anywhere on the road.

A scarf is a unique case, and it's difficult to find another item that has more than a few functions. However, convertible pants are a perfect example of useful clothing that is manufactured to be multipurpose. These have a zipper about halfway down so you can remove the bottom portion and turn them into shorts or capris. If you can find a comfortable pair that fits you well, they'll likely be invaluable during your trip. We especially liked using them during travel days when it was warm outside but cool inside the bus, train, or airplane.

The pair Tara used had a loose fit, allowing her to wear a layer underneath when we were in colder climates. Mike found another great use for them when we were on a boat. A few people were asked to hop out when we got to shallow water to help pull the boat to shore. Instead of having to roll up his pants like the other people who helped, Mike simply zipped off the lower portion and was able to avoid wet bottoms!

When thinking of how you can make the clothes you bring multipurpose, do remember that you will sometimes want to blend in with the locals, as it will make for a better experience. For example, some cultures around the world carry a very conservative attitude when it comes to clothing choices. (Be sure to research your potential destinations to educate yourself.) A Western wardrobe of shorts and a sleeveless shirt will invite stares and perhaps disapproval. Female travelers will want to wear loose pants and longer shorts or capris as well as shirts that cover the shoulders, chest, and stomach when traveling through these countries. Similarly, when visiting a religious site, you should wear clothing that will show others you respect local customs. One easy way to "double-dip" is to bring the convertible pants we recommended earlier since they zip off near the knee and are a quick way to cover up when entering a conservative area.

The last of the three considerations when packing specifically for long-term travel is how long it will take your clothes to dry. Synthetic material is unbeatable because of its quick-dry properties. Not only is this clothing breathable, it also wicks away sweat and water to keep your skin as dry as possible. This means that these fabric types will also take less time to air-dry (indoors or outdoors) after you wash them, so you can pack them up or wear them again sooner. Synthetics like polyester and nylon have the distinction of not only drying quickly, but also being wrinkle resistant and lighter than most fabrics (silk and wool are natural alternatives, but tend to be more expensive). Consider this option for underwear, shirts, and shorts.

There are many quick-dry clothing options sold today, and some brands tend to be much more expensive than others. It might be tempting to buy a popular brand because of a reputation for high quality, but you should instead consider buying clothing that is inexpensive and easily replaceable. Even though you may take good care of your clothes, there's still the possibility of petty theft, permanent stains, snags and tears, and even forgetfulness on your part, perhaps hanging a shirt out to dry and forgetting to grab it before leaving the hostel. While it's certainly ok to splurge on items that will be useful for your trip, keep these unforeseeable possibilities in mind before making any expensive purchases.

Besides quick-dry clothes, there are two material treatment options you may want to investigate as well. First, clothes treated with permethrin, an insecticide engineered specifically for fabrics, are available at specialty stores. This added layer of protection is great for absent-minded travelers who forget to regularly apply insect repellent. Think of how useful this would be in malaria-ridden areas.

Similarly, there are also clothes that offer sun protection. While clothing material will naturally filter small amounts of ultraviolet rays from the sun, it's still possible to get a sunburn even if you're wearing a cotton t-shirt, for example. If you'll be traveling to countries along the equator, a UPF-rated (Ultraviolet Protection Factor) shirt may be a good investment to help protect your skin in addition to sunscreen. This type of fabric may block up to 98% of ultraviolet rays and will likely cost you 20 to 25% more because of it, so gauge your need with your wallet.

Don't forget your feet

Try as you might to wear only sandals for the entire trip, the reality is that you will probably wear socks at some point. If you plan to exercise on the road, you might consider bringing running socks. But thin running socks will not keep your feet warm in cold climates. If you plan to travel during winter or in a colder area, you might consider bringing wool socks for warmth. But if you went hiking, you wouldn't want to wear wool socks. As you can tell, packing a pair or two of socks for every possible situation can take up a lot of space. Keeping utility in mind, you'll want to find one type of sock that you can wear for different occasions.

You might think that cotton socks are the answer since they are generally inexpensive. However, even though clothes made out of cotton are fine for lounging around at home, they aren't ideal for a backpacker on the go since cotton retains moisture. This means that the second your socks get wet, you increase the chance of developing blisters.

We recommend trying lightweight and mid-weight hiking socks. Both are designed for heavy use, so the determining factor for which you purchase will simply be your personal preference for the sock's thickness (try on all socks options with the shoes you will take on your trip). If your feet tend to sweat a lot, though, you may prefer a thinner sock made out of synthetic material. By checking the label, you'll see if the sock is made of acrylic, nylon, spandex, or polyester – these are all great for wicking away sweat and drying quickly.

It's amazing that we have said so much about socks but are still not finished. One last consideration is to bring a pair of compression socks for long flights, bus journeys, or train rides. These socks are worn to help keep blood circulating and prevent blood clots in your legs while you are stuck in a seated position for hours. Ideally, you would move around every couple hours on long-haul trips anyway, but sometimes that is not easy to do or you may fall asleep for a few hours. Wearing compression socks during times like this will help aid circulation in your legs. Aside from that benefit, they are also lightweight, breathe well, and roll up small.

Find footwear that won't kill your feet

Like clothing and socks, it can be challenging to find ideal multipurpose footwear for an extended trip like this. A good way to start is by envisioning what you like to do when you travel, as well as what types of out-of-the-ordinary activities you think you may do. For example, will you be running, hiking, walking around each town you visit, or do you think you'll be watching waves crash instead of admiring skyline or mountaintop views? Narrow down what you think will be your main activities so you can see where shoes options overlap.

Let's talk about hiking boots. You may view them as a good option for both hiking and sightseeing, but remember that they are bulky and will take up precious space in your pack, not to mention adding weight. Before you buy them thinking they're the best option, consider how much actual hiking – not just trekking through hilly trails – you will realistically do. If you decide you truly want to do extensive hiking during your trip, then you will definitely need the support and durability of hiking boots. They are rugged, offer ankle protection (there's nothing worse than rolling your ankle on a trail), are thicker (meaning they are warmer), and more heavy-duty (which may protect you against insect and snake bites) than other options.

If you want to be active but think you'll see more cities than wooded trails, consider athletic shoes with gel or air cushioning. Running shoes might not be the ideal choice, as they won't have as much padding and all-day comfort as walking shoes. Trail runners, however, are a good option for those who might do a little hiking, some jogging for exercise, and extensive walking around town. Some are water resistant, too.

Once you buy shoes for your trip, start wearing them immediately to break them in before you get on the road. You don't want to be in the middle of a bike ride or walking around the Great Pyramids when a blister develops.

Shoes we packed

Tara: I packed trail shoes, plastic flip-flops, thicker-soled flip-flops, and a pair of slip-on closed-toe shoes. This mix ended up being perfect for me.

I put the most effort into finding the right sneaker (ultimately buying trail shoes) because I wanted only one pair that I could use for exercising, light hiking, and walking around town.

The plastic flip-flops were solely for the shower and water activities. I naturally prefer flip-flops to sandals or sneakers, so I knew I wanted another pair with thick soles that would last longer than the shower shoes. The pair I chose became my go-to shoes for a casual walk, hanging out around the hostel, and to wear when traveling between cities or countries. They didn't dry quickly, so I tried to avoid wearing them in water or while it was raining.

Finally, I had a pair of black slip-on shoes. These collapsed into flat little pancakes and took up less space than flip-flops. They were a comfortable alternative to sneakers and flip-flops and were mostly used as my "nice pair of shoes." There were a few times we found ourselves eating at nice restaurants or going to events that required non-backpacker clothes and therefore decent-looking shoes.

Mike: This was a tough choice for me. Before our trip, I was not a big fan of sandals. This was partially due to never owning any open-toed footwear tougher than a simple pair of flip-flops. Since we decided that our trip would be an endless summer, I began looking into heavy-duty sandals options. Upon trying on hiking sandals, I knew I found the perfect pair. The soles resembled the tread of a car tire and the straps were thick and seemed built to last. During our trip this pair of sandals took quite the beating, and now a few years later they still appear like I just took them out of the box.

Likewise, I wanted a pair of hiking shoes that could take the punishment our trip was going to dish out. The decision to opt for shoes versus boots was mostly based on weight. The aforementioned sandals did not take up too much room, but they were heavy, and I didn't want to add much extra weight as the result of my footwear choices. I decided on low-top hiking shoes that also doubled as my "nice shoes" and ended up lasting several years.

Initially, I was hoping that I could use the hiking shoes as running shoes as well, but the reality is that I sweat too much not to have a pair of dedicated running shoes. To try something new, I bought a pair of five-toed barefoot shoes. I loved that they were lightweight yet offered protection for various terrains, though the big selling point for me was that they were made of quick-dry material, so I could wash them frequently and not be too concerned about drying time.

Finally, I brought the obligatory cheap "I'd-rather-not-be-barefoot" shower flip-flops. I had to buy a few replacement pairs along the way since I wore out my original pair, then lost and left behind others.

Another must-pack item for hotel hoppers is a pair of shower shoes, like plastic flip-flops or sandals, that dry quickly and slip on easily. Besides the obvious use of wearing them in hostel showers, flip-flops do not take up much space and are easy to tuck into a day bag as a back-up pair of shoes. If your primary shoes get soaked walking through water, just having the option to change into a new pair of shoes will be a huge relief.

Flip-flops often become the primary type of footwear among backpackers. In a way, it makes sense. When you wear closed-toe shoes or sneakers, you usually have to wear socks. Wearing flip-flops will help cut down on the amount of clothes you have to pack and the amount of laundry you will have to do. They're inexpensive, too. So if you get a "blowout," when the plastic thong is ripped from the sole, you won't spend too much to replace them.

If you have extra room in your bag, consider packing sandals as well for casual activities. Compared to flip-flops, sandals have thicker soles, are more durable, and are not prone to blowouts. And they're a step above sneakers in that you don't need to wear socks with them.

Staying warm and dry

Now that you have a range of outfits assembled, it's a good idea to find a rain jacket to go with them. Remember to double-dip as much as possible. If you think you are going to be exposed to colder weather, find a warm jacket that is also waterproof or a rain jacket that allows you to zip in a warm liner. This will prevent you from packing both a waterproof jacket and winter coat.

Some regions have a rainy season and monsoon season, and trust us when we say that the term "monsoon" is not used lightly. When it rains, it seems like buckets of water are continuously dumped from the sky. If you get caught in one of these rainstorms, you will instantly wish you had a jacket to keep you from getting drenched. (Don't forget what we said about getting a rain cover for your pack, too!) Most of these regions are tropical in climate, so you luckily won't need a heavy jacket. If possible, opt for a lightweight jacket that rolls up small; this will allow you to carry it either on your person or in a day bag. There is nothing worse than getting soaked in a rainstorm while your jacket stays nice and dry in your hostel room.

When shopping for one, you'll notice that some materials claim to be waterproof while others say they are water resistant. The difference between the two is significant. Waterproof materials prevent any moisture from penetrating the surface, whereas water resistant items can eventually become saturated and waterlogged. The number of layers a rain jacket has determines its ability to keep water out. The fewer the layers, the less protection, but generally the less expensive the jacket. As layers increase, the durability of the jacket improves, but the price will be higher as well.

Try on all your options. You'll want to make sure the jacket has good air-flow circulation (it's not too hot when zipped up) and that you can comfortably wear the jacket on top of other layers in case you are in colder climates. Also, some are designed to have a loose fit while others are specifically designed for male or female body types. Make sure that any jacket you buy has a hood (some surprisingly do not) and at least a couple pockets so you can put away important items.

If you don't think you'll hit too many rainy seasons along your journey, then you can skip this purchase. The good news is that cheap ponchos are plentiful in most areas that experience torrential downpours, so you can always buy one at the last minute if you choose not to bring a jacket or get stuck without it. You can also pack one or two ponchos instead of buying a rain jacket if you'd prefer not to incur the added expense or give up more space in your pack. The negative side to ponchos is that you get what you pay for. Most are made of thin plastic, so you may only wear them a couple times before they rip or tear at the seams. Faced with the alternative of having no protection at all, they are a cheap, quick fix.

If you think you will be traveling in chilly temperatures, here are some tips for winter jackets. First, try to find a winter jacket that is waterproof. One solution is to buy a jacket that has a shell made of waterproof and breathable material. The most well-known brand name of this fabric membrane is called Gore-Tex® (another popular brand is eVent). Gore-Tex® is fabric treated with a moisture repellent, which prevents water from being absorbed. Since it is a treated material, the effectiveness of the repellent will diminish over time, but you should not have problems during a year or two of travel.

Once you have a waterproof shell, think about which type of insulation you want. The lightest and warmest insulation option is down (feathers from geese or ducks), but not if you couldn't find a waterproof shell. If you get the feathers wet, not only will it take a long time to dry, it also won't offer protection against the cold weather while it's wet. Insulation made out of synthetic fibers is another good option, and it's also water resistant and dries relatively quickly, though it's heavier than down. Finally, there is fleece. Fleece does dry quickly, but it's quite bulky and will take up more room in your pack than the other two options.

This multi-functional wardrobe you packed might be taking up more space than you hoped. One way to compress your clothes is to put them in packing cubes, or even in plastic bags that you can squeeze the air out of before sealing at the top. Even though doing this will help you organize the contents of your bag better and allow you to pack a few extra items, don't forget that you still have to carry around the weight of any additional things you pack.

To camp or save luggage space

Camping along the way may seem like a fun way to experience each destination and save money on accommodations, but it may also make it difficult to pack light. The gear required, such as a tent, sleeping bag, and ground mats, takes up a large amount of space, even when tightly rolled. Then you must consider the less obvious items to pack – everything from travel pillows to cutlery to water purification tablets or filters. A seemingly innocent desire to go a more rustic direction can wreak havoc on your packing process – and the body carrying all this extra weight. This isn't to say it's impossible to camp during an around-the-world trip, but if it's something you want to pursue, consider making your camping destinations some of the first you visit. By scheduling them earlier in your itinerary, you can bring an extra bag packed with the necessary equipment. Then you won't have to stress yourself out by wondering where to purchase items on the road. After you're done camping, you can donate the equipment to a charity, a hostel, other travelers, or even box it up and send it to a friend or family member back home.

 When it makes sense to carry more luggage

Iceland was the first stop on our RTW. We rented a vehicle so we could drive the Ring Road on our own pace and explore as much of the island as possible. Upon seeing the cost of hostels, hotels, and, well, everything, we figured that camping would be a fun and inexpensive alternative. Since we would be there in early June, our research told us that camping sites would be open and available for a nominal fee.

A second piece of checked luggage was included in the price of our tickets, so we took full advantage by filling an additional bag with camping and winter-weather gear. We didn't plan to continue traveling with the bag and its contents after leaving Iceland (we were actually going to donate these items before leaving the United States if we didn't bring them to Iceland). So after our two weeks driving around the country and using our additional belongings, we gave our equipment to a woman and her daughter in Reykjavík whom we couch-surfed with for a couple nights.

We did, however, hold on to a few winter-weather clothes for our next two destinations (Finland and Russia). Then we ditched them when we hit warmer weather.

Accessories, extras, and other necessary items

Now that we've discussed some of the larger items, let's dive into the smaller — but no less important — things to consider bringing.

A silk travel sheet is a top recommendation from both of us. It's basically a sleeping bag liner that rolls into the size of a pair of bundled socks. It's not something you would camp with instead of a sleeping bag or rely on to keep you warm at night. Think of it as a protector from suspect sheets in a budget hotel or on an overnight train. Slipping into one of these will give you peace of mind and go a long way in helping you fall asleep. Not only are they a cocoon for your body, but many also have a space for pillow insertion, so you don't have to worry about your head touching pillowcases that look like they haven't been washed lately.

Silk liners aren't cheap, though. They're sold online and at outdoor stores, making them difficult to track down on the road. Therefore, you should consider making this purchase while you're still at home. Even though they're pricey, they are still worth the cost. We encountered dozens of dirty-looking sheets during our 14-month trip that made us pull our liners out. They ended up being one of the most-used items we packed.

Unless you plan to stay in four-star hotels for the entirety of your trip, it is important to pack a towel. We're not talking about an ordinary beach or bath towel, though. Those are heavy and large and take too long to dry. The solution? A quick-dry towel (again, sold online and at outdoor stores). These towels are usually made of a microfiber blend that distributes moisture across the towel's surface to speed the evaporation process. (The larger the towel, the more surface area, which therefore means that larger towels dry even faster.) Some also offer UV protection and are antimicrobial, discouraging the growth of bacteria.

Likewise, don't expect hostels to provide you with toiletries. You should consider packing the basics (toothpaste, toothbrush, soap, hair products, and so forth), but don't go overboard by bringing large sizes. You may be tempted to bring a big bottle of your favorite brand of conditioner, but consider how much you will use – perhaps only a pea-sized amount a few times a week. Instead, pack a travel-size container and simply buy more as you run out. You'll be able to easily find basic toiletries all over the world. Small containers will also fit better inside your day bag, so you can have them with you while you walk around town or are on a bus, plane, or train.

 ## If you like using tampons, consider bringing them with you

Boys, sit this one out. We're talking tampons here. Girls, listen up. While pads are pretty accessible around the world, tampons (especially your favorite brand) can be more difficult to find.

When we were in India, I learned that tampons can only be found in major cities, but even then they are difficult to locate. When I searched for tampons in Thailand and Vietnam, the only ones I could find were the kind without an applicator. In some countries, tampons with cardboard applicators are available, but it might be difficult or impossible to locate tampons with plastic applicators.

If you aren't a fan of wearing pads, I highly encourage you to pack a healthy supply of your favorite tampon for your trip. They do take up a lot of luggage space, but you'll be glad you did if home ends up being the last place you see them in stores.

While basic toiletries are easy to buy on the road, you may have difficulty finding specialty or medicated products, as well as your favorite brands in general. If you have trouble finding a particular product in your own country, expect that it will be even more difficult to acquire on the road. Do your research. If you can't find the answer online, consider using social media to find someone who lives in a particular country and ask them if a product is available there.

If you take medication regularly, stock up as much as possible. You may not be able to locate certain medication on the road, or you may find that the dosage or potency isn't quite the same. It's better to be safe than sorry, so even though a year's supply of pills will take up a lot of space in your pack, it will be worth the advance planning.

Entertaining yourself on the road

A laptop, smartphone, or e-reader will certainly keep you entertained, but if you're looking to limit your time with electronics, consider bringing some "old-fashioned" games with you. There are a variety of travel-sized card and board games that can keep you entertained and take up little space in your bag. Not only will you be able to play with your travel partner, but these games are also great for social settings (like at hostels, bars) and for making new friends. (Be careful when playing cards and games with dice, as some countries may have them outlawed or could mistake your playing for gambling.)

If you don't end up bringing a game from home, keep an eye out on the road for local games. While in Malawi, we found that the locals are known for their woodcarving skills, so we had a popular board game, called Bao, custom-made for us. It folded to 11" x 3.5" x 1.25" and was worth the small space it took up. Bao ended up being a conversation starter every time we pulled it out, and we ended up teaching the game to fellow travelers and playing with them.

Speaking of people you meet on the road, how will you stay in touch with them? Instead of always having to search for a pen and paper, just bring business cards to hand out. Before leaving, we decided to make business-like cards with our contact information. They included our names, email address, blog URL, and social media account handles. Instead of scrambling for a piece of paper and jotting down a name or email address, we were always prepared with a card, which is much more memorable than a napkin scribbled with illegible handwriting. There are many companies that print business cards inexpensively, so it won't break your budget to get a couple hundred made (Yes, you may need that many!). These cards will take up little space in your bag, and it's worth the effort for potential friendships that may last the rest of your life.

 Packing list, sans electronics

The following is a near-exhaustive list of everything we recommend that RTW travelers bring (minus electronics). We used all of these items during our trip, either having brought them with us initially or picked them up on the road. There are additional things we bought while traveling but left off this list (instant coffee packets, spices for cooking, and the like) since they aren't necessary to travel with. This may seem like an incredibly long packing list, but you would be amazed by what you can fit into an oversized backpack and day bag. Again, some of these items we didn't initially bring, and others were only with us for a short amount of time before we left them behind for other travelers.

Toiletries

- ☐ Bandana
- ☐ Body soap with a travel container
- ☐ Cotton swabs
- ☐ Feminine sanitary products
- ☐ Floss
- ☐ Hairbands (for those with long hair)
- ☐ Hairbrush
- ☐ Hand sanitizer or sanitary hand wipes
- ☐ Lip balm
- ☐ Lotion
- ☐ Mouthwash
- ☐ Napkins or tissues
- ☐ Quick-dry towel
- ☐ Razor
- ☐ Shampoo and conditioner
- ☐ Toiletry bag
- ☐ Toothbrush and toothpaste
- ☐ Travel toilet paper roll
- ☐ Washcloth

First Aid

- ☐ Anti-diarrhea tablets
- ☐ Antihistamine cream and pills
- ☐ Antiseptic wipes
- ☐ Aspirin
- ☐ Bandages
- ☐ Blister treatment
- ☐ Cold/flu medication
- ☐ Fine-point tweezers (for splinters)
- ☐ Powdered electrolytes (for rehydration)
- ☐ Required personal prescriptions
- ☐ Throat lozenges
- ☐ Topical antibiotic ointment
- ☐ Upset stomach relief tablets

Other Necessities

- ☐ Bag for dirty clothes
- ☐ Cards printed with your name and contact info
- ☐ Clothesline/extra shoelaces and a few clothespins
- ☐ Combination or key-accessible locks for your bags
- ☐ Driver's license and international driver's license
- ☐ Eye cover and earplugs

- ☐ Foreign currency, credit card(s), and ATM card
- ☐ Inflatable travel pillow
- ☐ Insect repellent
- ☐ Laundry soap
- ☐ Passport and passport-sized photos for visas
- ☐ Photocopies of important documents; password-protected jump drive of scanned image files
- ☐ RFID-blocking passport holders and RFID-blocking sleeves for credit cards
- ☐ Rubber sink stopper (for hand-washing laundry)
- ☐ Sewing kit (travel-sized)
- ☐ Silk travel sheet
- ☐ Small flashlight or head lamp
- ☐ Sunscreen
- ☐ Waterproof or water-resistant day bag

Nice to Have
- ☐ Bottle opener
- ☐ Cable or bike lock (for locking bags together or to a post in your hostel room or on a train)
- ☐ Carabiners
- ☐ Forks
- ☐ Games (travel-sized)
- ☐ Manila envelopes (for important documents)
- ☐ Money belt
- ☐ Plastic container for food
- ☐ Pocket knife
- ☐ Quart-sized sealable plastic bags (for food or keeping small items together)
- ☐ Small binoculars

Clothes
- ☐ Bathing suit
- ☐ Bras and sports bra
- ☐ Conservative clothing for traditional destinations
- ☐ Jacket or hoodie (for cool or cold weather)
- ☐ Jeans and other pants
- ☐ Pajamas
- ☐ Rain jacket
- ☐ Scarf
- ☐ Shirts and tank tops
- ☐ Shoes (shower shoes, sneakers, sandals, etc.)

☐   Shorts and skirts
☐   Socks
☐   Underwear

These are items that you could bring, but what about those you shouldn't? It kind of goes without saying that you need to leave expensive and expensive-looking items at home, like rings, necklaces, earrings, and watches. Wearing these items will make you look like you have money, which will make you a prime target for beggars and thieves. We even bought inexpensive wedding bands just for our RTW and left our nice rings at home.

Protect yourself

You may not worry much about mosquitoes at home, but in other parts of the world they are carriers of diseases like malaria and Japanese encephalitis. To protect yourself, always carry – and use – insect repellent. Even if you never seem to get bitten, it's always best to apply repellent to help decrease your risk of contracting one of these debilitating diseases. Repellent options fall into three categories: topical repellents made from DEET, Picaridin, or plant-derived ingredients. We recommend DEET because of its potency – it's supposed to last several hours – and therefore its overall effectiveness to keep mosquitoes away. Picaridin is a synthetic repellent made to resemble a natural compound that is found in plants that produce black pepper. It's expected to last about the same length of time as DEET. Natural repellents, however, need to be reapplied every hour or two to maintain their effectiveness.

Do take care when using DEET, as it can damage rubber, plastic, leather, and elastic materials – and there may be harmful side effects for long-term use of a highly concentrated repellent. If you are combining mosquito repellent with sunscreen, apply sunscreen first, wait 15 minutes, and then use the bug repellent. And of course, always wash your hands after application, especially before you eat.

 ## Ant-B-Gone!

Although insect repellent is good for keeping away mosquitoes, gnats, and other bothersome bugs, it won't keep ants at bay. Ants are insanely resilient, and once they get inside your room or possessions, there's almost no stopping them from crawling all over.

In Southeast Asia in particular, a smaller type of ant seemed to love getting into our electronics, so be careful. Two possible solutions are ground coffee beans and ground cinnamon. Apparently ants hate both of these. You can't store your laptop in coffee grounds, but sometimes making a ring around your bag is enough to keep them away.

Keep all food tightly sealed and separate from your bags. Whenever possible, hang a bag that contains your food separate from a bag that contains your electronics and any other items that ants shouldn't be getting into. This will make it tough for them to detect and gain entry.

Sunscreen is an equally vital part of your packing list. While it is widely available around the world, be sure to pick up a product that offers both UVA and UVB protection. Both UVA and UVB forms of ultraviolet rays can damage your skin, though in different ways. Most sunscreen that offers protection against both rays will call this out on the front label. Sometimes companies will tout their product as having broad-spectrum protection, and these are the types of sunscreen you will want to buy. Another consideration when purchasing sunscreen is the scale called Sunburn Protection

Factor (SPF). The higher the number, the higher the protection the sunscreen offers.

Also, some products are labeled as waterproof, but this claim is said to be exaggerated, and you should still reapply the cream every 40 to 80 minutes. Don't feel the need to bring a gallon with you before you leave, but do be aware of the type you should purchase when you are ready to buy and subsequently restock.

Balancing need and want in your pack

As you begin to purchase trip supplies, you may find that you have more to pack than you initially expected. With clothes, toiletries, and everything in-between, you should always draw the line between want and need. Everything comes down to two factors: "Can this be purchased on the road?" and "Does this have multiple uses?" Apply these criteria to questionable items and it should help you pack lighter.

Another trick to help you pare down is to do packing tests as your departure date nears. You may be a month away from leaving, but pack up everything you intend on taking with you as if you were heading out tomorrow. Then, walk around the block with your pack and see how you feel – yes, literally! Are you exhausted, or is the weight ok? Treat this test seriously and you may save yourself the headache of deciding what to toss out at the last minute.

This test may also help you and your travel partner realize that you need to redistribute the weight between the two of you. Aside from the obvious individual items (like clothes), group shared items together and split up who carries what. For example, in an effort to equally divvy up weight and volume, Mike packed our electronics and Tara carried the majority of our toiletry, first aid products, and food-related items (like sewing kit, pills, forks, spices). In addition to not weighing down the other person's pack, this also made it easier to track something down when we needed it.

 Items we never used on our trip

While we like to think we didn't pack excessive items, there were a few we carried around the world for 14 months and still never used. If any of these make it to your packing list, think long and hard about whether they are worth the effort:

- **Doorstop**: We heard this would help keep intruders out of sketchy hostel rooms. The idea is to wedge it under the door or between the door and the doorframe on the inside of the room. There were a few times we tried to use it, but it didn't fit in either space.
- **SteriPEN**: We did attempt to use it once in Africa, but it failed to work. It either got crushed in our bag or didn't work because of a manufacturing error. While on the road, we learned about the LifeStraw, which is inexpensive, doesn't require batteries, and overall seems like a more worthwhile option for your money.
- **Rechargeable batteries for the SteriPEN**
- **Funnel-filter for Vapur reusable bottles**: The purpose was to funnel contaminated water into our bottles without allowing the water to touch the rim of the bottle, where you drink from. Since our SteriPEN didn't work and therefore couldn't decontaminate the water we poured into our bottles, we had no use for this item.
- **Mylar emergency blankets**: Since we planned to camp in Iceland, we wanted to be extra prepared in case it got very cold at night. While we're glad we had these, we still never used them.

After drawing the line between want and need and test-packing your bag, lay out everything that you want to bring. Then cut it in half. Remove half the toiletries, half the clothes – everything! Then, double your money. Seriously. This is the top tried-and-true traveler packing tip.

It's natural to want to pack everything you'll possibly need during your trip. However, doing so makes it very easy to overpack, though it's not a big deal if you do. You'll know within the first few days of carrying your bag if you have more than you can handle. It's ok to leave things behind while you're on the road. The contents of your luggage can and should change throughout your trip as you get a feel for what you need and what wasn't necessary to bring.

CHAPTER IN REVIEW

❑ Find a perfect pack. Try on a few and walk around the store with heavy items inside the bag to get a feel for each. If they're expensive, you don't have to buy them in-store. Feel free to find one online, but do try them out in-person before making this expensive purchase.

❑ When figuring out what to pack, focus on utility. Take into consideration color, multi-purpose items, and drying time to maximize everything you bring.

❑ Find the right combination of footwear (don't forget shower shoes!) and break them in before you depart.

❑ Buy backpacker-specific items like a silk sheet, quick-dry towel, travel-sized games, and business cards with your personal contact information.

❑ Be firm about drawing the line between want and need when it comes to packing. If you need to, enlist the help of your travel partner like you did when you were reducing your possessions months ago.

❑ Lay out everything you want to bring, then cut it in half and double the amount of cash.

CHAPTER 9

How to Choose Electronics for the Road
3 Months Prior to Departure

YOUR TRIP WILL truly test the durability of the electronics you bring. Sand, rain and humidity, and shakes and vibration are just a few of the conditions they'll likely be exposed to. Manufacturers aren't necessarily making products with an RTW in mind, so you'll need to decide whether the equipment you already own is up for the challenge or if you have to budget in trip-specific upgrades. We encourage you not to spend money that you don't need to spend, but if you think that something you own won't last through your trip, research alternative devices to make an informed final decision.

For those of you who don't already own electronics you want to bring, or if you feel that what you currently have is outdated, we created guidelines that can help you buy only what you need depending on the type of traveler you are. We excluded brand- and model-specific recommendations in this chapter, and that's on purpose. Technology advances at such a rapid pace that it's difficult to recommend specific features and even devices, as they'll likely be outdated within a year or two.

That said, you don't need the newest, top-of-the-line devices for your trip either. The reason for this is simple: cameras that produce the best-quality images or videos, for example, often have more moving parts and are therefore more susceptible to damage. Think about a camera that has a removable lens. Humidity can enter the camera's body through that space and ruin a circuit. During your research, focus on trip-specific criteria, like durability, a waterproof exterior, and a shockproof interior.

Loss and theft are two more reasons to avoid buying the most expensive equipment. These are definite possibilities no matter where you are in the world, and if either happened, you would feel better knowing that you hadn't spent a whole paycheck on the device. Keep all of these factors in mind as you read this chapter and think about which electronics you might bring.

Write what you want, then figure out what you need

It's time to do something you've become accustomed to by now: make a list. We want you to think about which electronics you would purchase if the price tag didn't matter and what you would ultimately bring if you had plenty of space in your luggage. Scour the world of electronics for everything you think will make you happy. At this stage, don't get hung up on brands, models, or prices. Think in broad strokes and also consider devices you use now that you may want on the road.

Be realistic, though. Obviously a desktop computer is out of the question, so you will have to settle for a laptop, netbook, or tablet.

Travelers should always have a way to record memories, so you should definitely write down a camera and perhaps a stand-alone video camera if you enjoying shooting videos. Books are heavy, so write down an e-reader if you plan to read often. Don't forget a music-playing device for the times you don't want to read but still want to be entertained. Finally, think about the activities you participate in that would require an electronic device. For example, if you plan to drive, hike, camp, or do some off-the-beaten path exploring, you might consider bringing a GPS [global positioning system] receiver that is not tied to a phone network. And speaking of phones, you may want to bring an international phone for emergencies as well. Don't forget to add all the accessories that support the devices, like cases, batteries, power cords, memory cards, and an additional lens or two.

 ## Our (unrealistic) electronics wish list

To help you think of potential items for your wish list, we came up with our own. Here are examples of devices to consider for your trip:

- ❑ Laptop (with case and charging cable)
- ❑ Smartphone (with case and charging cable)
- ❑ Small, portable music player (with earbuds and charging cable)
- ❑ Noise-canceling headphones (with batteries)
- ❑ E-reader (with charging cable)
- ❑ GPS receiver (with charging cable)
- ❑ DSLR camera (with case, charger, and backup batteries)
- ❑ Telephoto and wide-angle lenses
- ❑ Waterproof video camera (with backup batteries and charger)
- ❑ Electronic toothbrush (with charging cable)
- ❑ Hair clippers (with charging cable)
- ❑ Hair straightener
- ❑ External hard drive (with case and cables)
- ❑ Travel alarm clock
- ❑ Travel immersion water heater

As you can see, this lengthy list is unrealistic for a long-term backpacking trip. Some items can be viewed as luxuries (like the noise-canceling headphones) and easily removed from the list. Others can be crossed off completely if you're able to bring a device with multiple functions. For example, a smartphone can also be used for music, as an alarm clock, and as an e-reader (if you don't mind reading teeny tiny text). By writing down all potential options, though, you are able to more easily differentiate the must-have items from the excessive, as well as think about why you wrote down these "excessive" devices in the first place.

In some ways, this activity is the opposite of what you have been training yourself to do in order to downsize your life. The ultimate purpose here, though it might seem counterintuitive, is to help you reduce the amount of devices you ultimately pack. By inflating your wish list to include everything you would want to have if size, weight, and price were not considerations, you ensure you think of everything you might want or need. You can begin to reduce it once you have a complete list, but at least you don't start with a reductionist attitude and forget to list something that might come in handy.

When the time comes to narrow the list down, be thorough and practical. Perhaps you use an electronic toothbrush and hair clippers at home, but for the sake of saving space and reducing the weight of your pack, consider using only a plastic toothbrush and disposable razor while you're on the road. For bathroom electronics in particular, don't forget that voltage isn't the same across the world. A blow dryer or hair straightener may work just fine at home, but if you need to buy a down-converter box in order to use a device in another country, eliminate it from your list. A down-converter box is bulky and heavy, which does not describe the things you should be packing, especially if the only benefit is to power another device that might also be unnecessary (we'll touch on down-converter boxes again when we discuss voltage later in this chapter).

It should be somewhat easy to identify items that you can cross off completely, like those just mentioned above, and you may be able to creatively combine others. For example, instead of packing both a wide angle and a telephoto lens, decide on a lens that splits the difference, like one that has an optical zoom but is not too large. Lenses are fragile and prone to damage through dust, vibration, and moisture (conditions you are bound to experience during an RTW). While having a spare lens may provide you with more versatility when snapping shots, weigh the risk of damage and hassle of carrying additional weight versus the frequency of how often you would actually change out lenses.

Continue to look for ways to reduce redundancies, extending this idea to device capabilities as well. For example, if your smartphone's location services works internationally, this may mean you will not have to buy a GPS navigation device. And if you're happy with a point-and-shoot camera, you could just use the camera on your smartphone as your main camera.

The last thing to consider when narrowing down your device list is which additional items you will need to pack to accompany the devices you plan to bring. Some of the things on your list may seem both important and small size-wise, but when you add in their accessories, they may not be worth it after all. It's obvious that batteries, power cables, and memory cards are useful and necessary, but consider the items that may be required but not so obvious. For example, an immersion water heater is a great tool if you want to save money by making your own warm beverages and cups of soup, but you will need a heat-resistant cup when you want to use it. These cups may not always be accessible, and you wouldn't want to buy a new one at every stop on your itinerary.

Will you have room in your bag to pack the immersion heater and a cup? In the end, you may decide that it's not worth the money you save. Plus, you can always pick up items during your trip if you decide you really should have brought something.

Once your list is complete after removing all superfluous items, don't jump into buying anything just yet. Read on to learn about what features you should research, why voltage matters, and which accessories to consider purchasing as well. Then, the final thing to do before you make an electronics purchase is read any and all reviews. It is easy to get swept up in a sales pitch, especially in the build-up to your trip's departure, and make impulse purchases or purchases that aren't well thought out. If a product is good, you should be able to find lots of positive feedback. But if a product has issues, you will definitely read about those as well.

Finding the right computer

Now that you've narrowed down your list of electronics, the next step is to decide whether to buy brand new products or to bring the ones you already own. You will likely use most devices on a daily basis, so you need items that you are comfortable with and will also last throughout your trip (or at least as long as possible).

A computer, if you choose to bring one, will likely be the largest and perhaps the most expensive item in your pack. Plenty of travelers do not bring their own computer during trips, but this means you'll have to give up privacy and control for the times you do want to jump online. The first and foremost concern for using public computers is security. If you plan to check your finances while you're traveling, you should definitely consider the benefits of using your own private device. It is too easy to have your information compromised on public computers by spyware.

Megawatts, gigahertz, gesundheit

As you shop around for a personal computer, there are a few terms that you will definitely see on the specifications sheets. You should not only be aware of them, but also understand how they relate to your potential purchase. Here are those common terms and their definitions:

- **Display resolution**: This is measured in pixels. Image quality will be better on computers with a higher number of pixels.
- **Processor speed**: This is measured in gigahertz (GHz). The higher the number, the faster the speed of the computer.
- **Random-access memory (RAM)**: This is measured in gigabytes (GB). The higher the number means that more complex programs can load and run faster.
- **Storage size**: This is measured in GB or terabytes (TB). The higher the number, the more files can be saved locally.

For those wanting to bring a personal computer, your options are laptops, netbooks, and tablets. To help narrow your decision, determine whether you want to bring a Mac or Windows-based computer. Then, think about what you will be doing on the computer. If you will only use it for word processing, simple photo editing, and Internet connectivity, then there is no reason to pay for a top-of-the-line model. On the other hand, if you plan to do graphic design creation, video editing, and processor-intensive projects, then you need a model that will be able to handle your demands.

What helps ground a major purchase like a laptop are the practical factors of cost, size, weight, and specifications. A typical netbook is small and light, connects to the Internet, performs basic tasks, and is fairly inexpensive. A souped-up Dell laptop or MacBook Pro can be blazingly fast and capable of running any and all programs, but heavy, large, and very expensive. Even though they are amazing machines, you should be buying according to your needs and skills, not according to your hopes and dreams. So if you lack the knowledge and skills to use video- or photo-editing programs, then you likely won't be able to learn them on the road. Being realistic in this way will also help save you money.

If you opt to bring a laptop, two things you will want to keep in mind are how you will protect it from theft and the elements. When it came to keeping our laptop safe while on the road, we chose not to bring it out in public whenever possible and also referred to it as "LT." (As in, "Do we need to bring the LT?") It's a very basic code name, but by using it, it's likely that others didn't know what we were talking about and therefore didn't know we were traveling with a laptop. Additionally, think about purchasing a protective fitted case or carrier to help safeguard your investment. Especially if you opt for a less-rugged computer (i.e., a plastic-housed computer), getting a case that snaps on will give you the extra protection that may make a difference if an accidental drop occurs.

 Our eyes were larger than our backpacks

A couple months before we left, we fell in love with a 15" MacBook Pro in an Apple store. We had several criteria that it seemed to fulfill. I wanted it to be small enough not to be unwieldy and also so it was easy to take out where it wouldn't be too conspicuous in a public place. Besides feeling like a good size and weight, it also had the right specifications for memory and storage for photo and video editing. As an added bonus, you could replace the battery yourself (a nice feature considering other models require you to send the computer off to be serviced). We ordered one with pumped-up specifications and an extra battery and were very excited about it. Then it arrived in the mail and we lifted up the box. "Wow," I thought, "this seems really heavy. Maybe it's just extra padding for shipping purposes?" Once we took it out of the box, we found that the packaging was not adding too much weight, but that the computer was actually that heavy.

Clearly, the heft of the laptop combined with the extra battery made it obvious they should not come with us, but what were we to do? Luckily, the Apple store exchanged it for a 13" MacBook Pro, which ended up being an even better size and weight for our RTW. But by getting a smaller-sized laptop, we lost processor speed and overall storage size, which meant that it sometimes took hours to render a video. However, overall, the few things we lost by downsizing were made up for by the smaller size and weight. While it was not an ideal situation, this just illustrates the importance of getting electronics early enough so you can test them and make alterations, exchanges, or returns if needed.

Buying a phone that will work abroad

The next item to consider bringing on your trip is a smartphone. The main advantage that a smartphone has over a basic phone is its data capability. If you need to quickly search for your hotel's address or plot it on a map, you can easily connect to Wi-Fi or your cellular network and eliminate the need to pull out your laptop or tablet. As smartphones continue to grow in power, size, and utility, the need for a standalone computer for an extended trip is starting to diminish, though it does depend on how you plan to use it. However, while the need for a computer may be in flux, the importance of carrying a cell phone on the road cannot be overstated. Beyond the safety factor, having a phone while traveling provides a means of booking reservations, communicating with locals, and having a phone number that friends and family can instantly reach you on (versus only being available via email).

The country you live in will undoubtedly affect your outlook toward phones. Specifically, those who live in the United States and those who live nearly anywhere else in the world will have differing experiences with cell phone service. Most telecommunication providers outside of the United States do not require contracts and instead operate on a pay-as-you-go model. However, wireless telephone providers in the United States predominately operate on a contract model where free or discounted phones are given to customers who sign a one- or two-year contract. Those who break their contract while it's still valid are required to pay the remaining cost of their "free" or discounted phone, depending on the amount of time left on their initial contract. Keep this in mind if you're a U.S. resident and planning to sign a new contract soon. If it overlaps with your RTW, will you cancel it or keep it? Some providers offer international text and data plans, but if you don't have international coverage, there may not be a benefit in continuing to pay a monthly bill. However, if your contract is almost over, it might be cheaper to pay off those last few months instead of paying the remaining cost of a discounted phone you received.

Another major concern for a phone you already have, or are thinking of purchasing for your trip, is which type of network the device can function on. Luckily, there are only two types: CDMA and GSM. There isn't much of a need to discuss the intricate details of these two technologies, but it is important to know that a majority of U.S. carriers use CDMA and a CDMA-based phone will not work on a GSM network and vice versa. You may think, "Great! A majority of U.S. carriers use CDMA, so I should be set abroad." Sadly, you'd be wrong, as most other countries use GSM.

Since most of the world's mobile carriers use GSM networks, you can take any GSM-compliant phone, pop in a SIM card, and start making calls. A SIM card is a tiny microchip that carries basic information (like your contacts) and that identifies your phone to cell phone towers by using the telephone number on the card. So let's say you buy a basic $15 USD Nokia phone in Finland. Without a SIM card, you may be able to make emergency calls, but that's it. In order to make and receive non- emergency calls, you must purchase a SIM card, insert into your phone, and add money to it. SIM cards can be purchased at most convenience stores and supermarkets. Every time you make or receive a call, money is deducted from your account balance. When you run out of money on your SIM card, all you have to do is buy credit from just about any general store or by calling the provider's customer service line. But let's say you leave Finland and travel to Turkey. Your Finnish SIM card won't work there, so you have to buy a Turkish SIM card and go through the same process to add money. Once you purchase credit for the new SIM card, your phone will be activated for non-emergency calls and also have a new local telephone number.

It is incredibly easy and inexpensive to travel with a GSM phone and to buy a local SIM card when you arrive in a new country. So if you opt for a GSM smartphone, you'll not only be able to make calls, but also use the network for data and GPS for maps (dependent, of course, on the plan and mobile company you signed up for). It will certainly make your travel experience easier if you aren't dependent on Wi-Fi and could easily connect to your cellular network whenever you're in a service area.

There's also another cell phone option on the market called an international cell phone. The selling points are that they work in almost every country; use a single phone number; have no contracts, monthly fees, connection fees, or usage requirements; and you're only charged for the calls you make. The reason these phones aren't very popular is because the per-minute fees are very high compared with other options. So while an international cell phone would work as soon as you arrive in a country, you will pay a premium for every call you make. Weigh this option if you prefer convenience, the piece of mind of having a working phone the minute you land in a new country, or, on the flip side, if do not plan to use the phone frequently. However, if you end up staying in a country for a long period of time and plan to make a lot of in-country calls, it might be worth getting a domestic SIM card to save money and provide friends and businesses with a local phone number.

 You may soon be able to leave your camera at home

Cell phones are increasingly growing in power and capabilities. Specific to picture and video recording, they are starting to rival the quality of stand-alone cameras. However, their largest limitation so far has been optical zooming. DSLRs and single-body cameras with a retractable lens offer some amount of zoom versus nearly all cell phones, which only have a fixed lens. However, there are companies that now manufacture lenses that act as a fixed zoom lens and are specifically cut to fit certain phones. Even more impressive is the rise of new innovations that allow an automatic lens to be affixed to a mobile phone's camera and use Bluetooth technology to communicate with the phone to zoom and focus. This means there may be a point in the near future when your cell phone and detachable lens will be all you need to pack to record your memories on the road.

Our experience was an amalgam of new and old technologies. We already had an iPhone 4 under contract with a U.S. wireless telephone company, but it was a CDMA phone. Since it still had Wi-Fi capabilities, a working camera for stills and videos, and could play movies and music, we decided to suspend our contract and bring the phone with us. It's quite possible that we ended up using it more than any other device during our trip, often taking it out instead of more expensive devices like our camera or laptop. We used it to snap photos, refer to screenshots of maps or directions, and jot down expenses and reminders. Since it wasn't connected to a cellular network, it could not receive or make calls, so we picked up an inexpensive phone at our first RTW stop because we didn't bring one from home. The device we bought was basic but durable, and that was all we needed it to be. Its main purpose was for urgent uses or to call hostels or Couchsurfing hosts. It also served a secondary purpose of providing our family with an emergency number we could be reached at (especially in locations where we did not have Internet access). We bought new, relatively inexpensive SIM cards in almost each country we visited, and the phone functioned without fail for the duration of our trip.

Track your location and plot your route

A portable GPS unit is another electronic device you may want to consider packing. However, its usefulness to you is really contingent on the type of traveler you are and what you plan to do at the locations you visit. If you think you may hike or drive during your trip, it would be beneficial to carry a GPS to help with navigation.

On our trip, we didn't go on many solo hikes, but we did drive around Iceland. Since that was the only country we planned to drive in, we didn't purchase a GPS for our trip, but we did make sure to get one with our rental car. We heavily relied on it, and without it we may have gotten lost (actually, we definitely would have), and it (surprisingly) allowed us to be spontaneous during our drive. Since the GPS showed us how far we were from our next destination and the location of nearby hotels, we were able to take detours, stop earlier than planned, or continue farther if we wanted. It was well worth having; though if we had purchased one, it would have had diminished returns since we wouldn't have used it again.

Carefully consider how often you would use GPS during your trip, and leave it out if you don't think you'll be driving or hiking. If you think a GPS unit will be beneficial, make sure the one you purchase works internationally. Some units may work only in your home country or require you to purchase additional country maps.

Recording memories

This goes without saying, but we're going to say it anyway: You must bring a camera of some sort! This will undoubtedly be an important and unforgettable chapter in your life, and you should record as much of it as possible. You'll want to show family and friends the sights you saw, the people you met, the amazing food you ate, and even the dingy hostel you survived a night in. After your trip, you'll frame your favorite pictures, put some on rotation as your computer's wallpaper, and smile as you look through your albums and remember that amazing time in your life when you left everything behind to travel the world.

So what kind of camera should you pack? Be wary of bringing a top-of-the-line DSLR camera. These can cost several thousand dollars, and this fact does not go unnoticed by thieves. In some places, you might as well be wearing a gold chain around your neck. The nicest camera with the most megapixels probably isn't what you need for a trip like this anyway. Plus, the number of megapixels a camera shoots per image is irrelevant if you don't shoot at the highest resolution (and you probably wouldn't since those files would be very large).

DSLR cameras are a good option, as they have many benefits. They offer the best quality recording options for both still and video images and can shoot RAW images, meaning their resolution is on par with 35mm film. At this resolution, you can zoom into an image quite a bit before it looks pixelated.

If you decide to purchase a DSLR, there are a variety of accessories you may want to consider buying in order to take full advantage of the camera's potential. Some of these include an external microphone, portable lights or flashes, an electronic viewfinder, and cases for the camera and its accessories.

You'd think a DSLR camera would be the optimal choice for a trip like since the quality of the images they shoot is top-notch, but they actually receive failing marks when it comes to durability. By having so many moving parts, they are more apt to have problems. Everything – including but not limited to dust, sand, moisture, and sweat – is your enemy when it comes to potentially scratching your lens or getting water inside the camera's body.

Since DSLRs and cameras like them are so susceptible to many external factors, you may want to consider bringing a durable single-body camera with a fixed lens. (Be careful not to confuse this with cameras that have a retractable lens, as the lens on those cameras can easily be damaged.) Most camera manufacturers offer a model that is designed for tough conditions. These typically have a fixed lens, and their only outwardly moving parts are the doors for a battery and memory card. The top models continue to improve year after year by increasing the range of temperatures they can be exposed to, the distance they can be dropped without damage, and the number of feet the camera can be brought under water while staying waterproof. A camera that can be exposed to these extreme conditions should be appealing, but while you gain durability, you often lose image quality and have fewer options while shooting (like adjusting aperture and shutter speed).

 Terms to know when camera shopping

There are many good sales pitches out there that could easily persuade you to buy a camera model you don't need. A top-of-the-line camera isn't worth your money if you don't take full advantage of the features that differentiate it from a camera one step down. To help identify those differences and determine whether you need the features, review the terms in this section and then go camera shopping.

- **Aperture range**: This is how large and small the iris of your camera can open. The larger it opens, the more light it lets in, meaning that it can more easily take pictures in low-light situations. This also directly affects the depth of field your shots can achieve. Some cameras offer a manual aperture-adjustment feature while others are automatic.
- **Depth of field**: The scope of objects that are in focus. Pictures with most of the image out of focus have what is called a shallow depth of field (usually in darker situations). Images with a wide depth of field will have everything in sharp focus (usually in brighter situations).
- **Focal length**: This is the distance your lens can focus. Most cameras don't have a problem focusing on objects that are far away, but many have great difficulty with macro, or close-up, photography. A camera with an interchangeable lens will allow you to switch lenses so you can capture objects at a range of distances. (The problem, though, is that you would need to carry a variety of lenses, which can be heavy and take up a lot of space.)
- **Optical zoom**: This is the capability of your lens to zoom in to objects that are near or far away.
- **Digital zoom**: This is not true zoom. This is merely a digital enhancement, similar to the zooming function in an editing program.
- **Image stabilization**: Another digital feature that steadies the image or a video when the picture-taker's hands are shaky.
- **Facial detection**: Detects faces before exposing for the shot in order to adjust lighting for them.
- **GPS/Geo-tagging**: Uses a satellite to pinpoint your location

for the photograph. You can access this in your image's metadata. (Be aware that any digital enhancements and use of a GPS feature will rely heavily on your battery and therefore drain your battery power pretty quickly.)

Now that we have slammed DSLR cameras, you probably want to know what type of camera we used on our trip. We opted for an EVIL camera (EVIL stands for external viewfinder interchangeable lens). Think of it as DSLR-lite. It was lighter, more compact, and less conspicuous than most of the DSLR alternatives, while offering us the option to bring multiple lenses. The smaller body meant that we gave up a few features and settled for slightly lower image quality compared to cameras costing thousands more, but overall we felt like it was a good fit for us and our trip.

A great feature that most, if not all, digital cameras have is the ability to shoot video. Just about any digital camera can record video, therefore eliminating the need to purchase a stand-alone video camera. However, if you do intend to shoot a lot of video, you might want to consider purchasing a dedicated video camera along with your still camera (we did). Video requires a lot of power from most digital cameras, so you will likely find that your battery drains quickly in video mode. Likewise, some DSLRs have issues with overheating from continuous video recording and are unable to shoot for more than 15 to 20 minutes at a time. Rather than kill our main camera's battery to shoot the occasional video, we opted to purchase a durable, waterproof, shockproof video camera. Since we had two devices, we split responsibilities during our trip, turning Mike into our main videographer while Tara took most of our still images.

By bringing two devices, we were able to shoot concurrently, sometimes of the same thing, but at least capturing the shot that we each wanted. Since our video camera was more rugged than our still camera, we were able to record during situations when we felt uncomfortable bringing out our digital camera (like on sand dunes or in water). We did this knowing that later we could pull decent-quality still images from the video.

 ## When traveling, only let out of your sight what you can live without

Theft is not isolated to a certain country, region, or even airport. Make sure you are proactive when it comes to protecting your gear. Never check or put anything in a trunk that you cannot live without. When you go on flights, bus rides, ferries, or even taxi rides, always store your valuables in a bag that you keep attached to you like glue. In the shuffle of trying to catch your flight, it is all too easy to lose track of a bag. There are known scams where you load up the trunk of a taxi only to watch the driver speed off with your bags (to protect ourselves from this situation, we always had one of us loading or unloading luggage while the other person sat in the back seat). By having your travel partner's and your passports, electronics, and other important items in a day bag that you assign to one of you, you can be less paranoid about all of your bags and just make sure that the one bag never leaves your sight. And whatever you do, do not check this bag when you fly!

Be careful about going overboard with electronics, though. Not only will thieves take notice, but the government might as well. Going through customs with several cameras and lenses may raise some eyebrows and red flags in certain countries (they may wonder whether you're a reporter or, worse, a spy). Since we were carrying only two inconspicuous cameras, we were able to breeze through customs. Keep this in mind when surveying the final devices you choose to bring.

Volts and plugs

Second-tier items made up the remainder of our electronics wish list. We wanted to back up all of our digital memories, so we packed a hand-sized external hard drive with a protective case. Cosmetic devices like an electronic toothbrush, hair clippers, and hair straightener were important to us when we were making our list, so we made an effort to bring them as well (only the travel-sized hair straightener lasted the duration of our trip, and Tara was happy she brought it). However, the travel alarm clock and travel immersion water heater fell by the wayside. Our smartphone was able to handle the job of an alarm clock, and we determined that an immersion heater wouldn't get much use after our first destination, where we planned to camp.

With superfluous electronics removed from our list, the next step in the process – before making any purchases – was to make sure the electronics we already had would support different voltage outside of our home country. Admittedly, finding out what voltage your laptop, smartphone, or camera battery charger accepts is not a top priority. However, it takes only one instance of plugging an item into an outlet with the wrong voltage to fry your device. Luckily, most electronics manufactured today are done so with international standards in mind and are either dual voltage (allowing the user to flip a switch to match the desired country's voltage) or multi-voltage (meaning it can automatically accept 110-240 volts, which is the full range of voltage used).

To use single-voltage electronics (those that can only operate on 110 volts or 240 volts) in countries that use a different voltage, you would need to buy a down- or up-converter box. We strongly advise against this since these boxes are quite heavy. It would be worthwhile to simply replace your single-voltage electronics with ones that are dual voltage or multi-voltage.

Voltage isn't the only thing to keep in mind when plugging in your devices. Currently, there are 9 types of sockets in the world. Luckily, there is a very simple solution. We recommend purchasing a travel-sized power strip that supports the outlet configuration of the electronics you have and then buying only one adaptor for each new region you visit (just ensure that the power strip is multi-voltage). Insert your power strip into the plug adaptor, then the adaptor into the wall's outlet, and you will have just multiplied your available sockets without needing multiple adaptors. If you are the forgetful type, use electrical tape to connect your adaptor and power strip together to prevent you from leaving the adaptor plugged into the wall when you're done.

Travel power strips are indispensable. Some even come with USB outlets, which make them an even greater asset. There were times when our power strip was charging four devices at a time, freeing us up to focus on other things instead having to watch over and rotate batteries and devices as they hit 100%.

 ### Trust me, I can manually brush my teeth

My electronic toothbrush and hair clippers survived the downsizing process, despite Tara's best efforts to get me to leave them behind. I was convinced the money I would save on protecting my teeth and cutting my own hair would justify taking it all. However, in order to use the devices abroad, I needed a voltage down-converter box, which I purchased in the weeks leading up to our departure.

When it came time to leave, I packed the converter box, hair clippers and all its attachments, and a toothbrush and extra toothbrush heads (I assumed I wouldn't be able to find any on the road). The weight of just these items was somewhere around 15 pounds and it took up a lot of space in my pack. Still, I was determined to take it all with me.

In our last 24 hours in the United States, we traveled from Washington, D.C., to New York City for our flight to Iceland. After carrying my pack on and off buses, in and out of taxis, and through the subway, I realized how foolish it would be to bring these extra items with me. They were definitely weighing me down. Luckily, I had time to run to a post office and mail them to my parents, as I couldn't bear just dumping them in the Big Apple.

Now, looking back, it's laughable how naïve I was. But it also illustrates just how important it is to do a packing test. If I had done one in D.C., I wouldn't have had to wait until New York City to realize I had overpacked.

More space for your memories

Perhaps you now have a camera or video camera in mind. The price and voltage are right, and it has all the features you want. Before you make any purchases, though, consider which accessories you may need or want. Some of these could be expensive, so it's important to factor in their cost as well.

One not-to-be-forgotten necessity for your camera and video camera is a memory card. It is best to buy at least two large-capacity cards so you always have a backup on hand if one becomes damaged or fills up. The size and cost of memory cards are directly proportional, with larger cards costing significantly more than those with a smaller storage capacity. But you do get what you pay for. You don't want to be on safari photographing elephants when your memory card fills up, then forced to scroll through images to decide which to delete to make room for your next shot.

To ensure that something like that doesn't happen anyway, we recommend creating a daily or weekly workflow of transferring photos and video to your laptop and external hard drive. You'll also want to create a naming or numbering scheme (identifying the media by location and date, for example) to prevent you from ending your trip with an unmanageable image library where you can't find what you're looking for. Additionally, a workflow like this will free up your cards to hold more images and videos while ensuring your footage is backed up. Then if your card does fail, you won't lose as many memories.

You likely won't need more than two cards per device if you have a good transferring system in place. If you do end up needing another card, though, memory cards are fairly easy to find on the road, so you don't have to worry about bringing many extras to begin with.

 Understanding memory card options

The most common memory cards are called Secure Digital, or SD cards. When you're shopping for an SD card for your devices, there are three key things you want to understand that will guide your purchase:

- **Physical size**: There are full-size SD, miniSD, and microSD cards. The one you need is based on the device you're using.
- **Storage size**: SD high capacity (SDHC) or SD eXtended capacity (SDXC) are your two options. SDXC formats are significantly larger and therefore can store much more footage than SDHC.
- **Class rating**: Ratings range from 1 to 10 and refer to the speed that information is transferred in megabytes. Class 1 will have the slowest transfers, while a class 10 will transfer the fastest, mostly used with professional-quality cameras.

Keeping your electronics powered

Batteries will be required for some of your electronics, and you'll have two choices: single-use or rechargeable. Single-use batteries are generally easy to find all over the world, so locating a replacement C battery to buy should not be difficult. If possible, opt for lithium batteries, as they are the lightest and most durable.

Another option, which is more expensive upfront, is to purchase rechargeable batteries for the electronics you know you will be using frequently. There are four varieties, all made with different metals and appropriate for varying types of electronics: nickel-metal hydride (NiMH), pre-charged NiMH, nickel-cadmium, and lithium-ion. Of the four types, lithium-ion batteries are preferable since they retain a charge the longest, yield the most charges overall, and perform well in most temperatures. They also make up the lion's share of the market and are therefore easy to find. (The main differences between lithium and lithium-ion batteries are that the former have a higher energy density and cannot be recharged. Lithium-ion batteries, however, were engineered to be rechargeable.)

One thing you may not be able to find easily on the road is a replacement proprietary battery. As we mentioned, the basic AA-, AAA-, C-, and D-sized batteries are easy to track down, but locating a GoPro Hero3 battery, for example, might be nearly impossible in some cities, and sometimes those that you do find may be counterfeit and therefore unreliable.

Once you settle on the devices you're bringing, test those that require a proprietary battery type to determine whether you want to purchase spare batteries. If you're concerned about their lifespan and do want to buy some spares, keep in mind that manufacturers' products will always be more expensive than generic knock-offs.

However, the latter will not have the same lifespan potential as the manufacturer's brand. We took a chance with our digital camera and purchased three spare "unofficial" batteries. During our trip, they were consistently unreliable, never holding as long a charge as the official battery did and over time losing their charge quicker and quicker. When our trip ended, after 14 months of use, only one of the spare batteries could still hold a charge while the manufacturer's battery is working just fine. As you can see from our real-life example, while you will surely save some money by purchasing a knock-off, you almost always give up reliability.

Some electronics, like smartphones and tablets, do not have easily removable batteries, so purchasing a spare wouldn't be your best option. For these devices, you'll want a way to charge them on-location if you're using the device and your battery drains without an outlet in sight. Here you have two solid options: solar chargers or an external power supply.

Solar power has been around for a while, and the technology has progressed to the point where portable cells are a viable source of power. If you choose this route, know that chargers that have more panels will be better than those with fewer since the larger surface area will capture more energy and fill the power supply more quickly. Some of these chargers have built-in batteries as well, allowing you to store the captured energy until you want to charge another device.

Storing captured energy for later use is essentially what an external power supply is, and that is your second charging option. An external power supply is a rechargeable battery, plain and simple. These stand-alone battery packs, sometimes called power banks, charge from AC power (wall outlets) and double as a power source when you do not have access to an outlet. You can expect that your device will charge at the same rate as if you had it plugged into a

USB or wall outlet. When shopping for battery packs, research the storage capacity, power output, and what material the battery is made of. The storage capacity will tell you how many times you can charge another device before this battery pack needs to be recharged. Knowing the power output is important because the power bank needs to produce voltage equal to or more than your device requires. This is why most battery packs can power phones or cameras but few can charge a laptop (the power output is simply not strong enough). Finally, the ideal material – as we've seen before – is the light and durable lithium-ion.

Software, security, and storage

With all the time and effort you've put into researching each device you want bring, you should make sure you're comfortable using all of them prior to leaving and have the proper protections in place to safeguard your investments on the road.

If you're bringing a computer, learn how to use any software you've loaded onto it if you're not already familiar with all the programs. However, you should avoid purchasing hundreds of dollars' worth of programs unless you're committed to learning them long before you leave. This is especially true of photo and video editing programs since they tend to be expensive and may take a while for you to learn. Start with trial versions to test the functionality and determine whether you even like using the program. Otherwise, it could be a big waste of money. (As an aside, make sure that all your software is up-to-date prior to departure. Since running updates can sometimes be time-consuming, you should finish as many installations as you can while still at home with reliable Internet.)

Another option is to seek out inexpensive, easy-to-navigate options and learn them when you buy them. You could try freeware or even cloud-based solutions (meaning they require an Internet connection in order to use them), though we would advise against the latter since Internet isn't guaranteed worldwide or at fast speeds when it is available. You should also keep this in mind for any video subscriptions (Hulu, Netflix, and Amazon Prime) you may hope to connect to while on the road.

You might be thinking, "Wait a second, subscription-based video services only work based on your IP address's current location. I probably can't connect to mine in certain countries." To that we would say, "Have you heard of a virtual private network (VPN)?" A VPN essentially creates a private network across public access. Every time you log into a wireless network, anyone can intercept and access the data you are sending and receiving. Every time you do online banking, enter sensitive information, or a type in a password on an unencrypted network, you are potentially opening up your data to theft. Many businesses require their employees to use a VPN in order to secure and encrypt their communications. Not only are the data secured, but the VPN service provider can alter your IP address's location. This fringe benefit of a VPN gives you the ability to watch or read country-specific web content. In other words, it allows you to bypass blocks that are in place in countries that may be controlling content or access. This is a very real issue that we encountered on the road. Certain governments block news outlets, social media, and other controversial websites. Through the company that hosts your VPN, you can designate the country that your IP address appears as. This means that when you're in a country that censors Internet content, you should be able to sign into your VPN and surf without restrictions (as long as your IP address's country allows it).

A VPN can protect the data you send and receive online, but what about protecting the data on your computer? Some smartphones come with a "find your phone" application that allows you to locate a lost or stolen phone, and there is similar software for computers.

This software essentially tracks your computer's location when you log into the Internet. The second your computer is lost or stolen, you just notify the software company, which can either delete your data (which is especially beneficial if you have confidential information saved) or track the location and alert the authorities. The stress of having your computer stolen is bad enough without having to worry that your personal information has been compromised, too.

Now that your computer is secure, you'll want to make sure you back up all the data you've been saving on it. You have two main options: cloud backup and physical storage. There are a variety of cloud storage options, although they typically come at a price for large amounts of storage space (you'd be charged on either a monthly or yearly basis). With cloud storage, you never have a physical home for your files because they are stored in cyberspace. The company you select will use servers to save your files, and as long as you have an Internet connection, you can upload new files or access old ones. Depending on the package you choose, either you will have to upload files manually or the system might auto-sync with your device when it's turned on and connected to the Internet. Another benefit besides accessibility is that your files are safe even if your devices are stolen (as long as you backed up everything).

The biggest disadvantage of cloud storage for a world traveler is the need to be tethered to a reliable Internet connection to back up your data. To us, this outweighs the benefits, especially when dealing with large video or image files since you are at the mercy of the Internet connection. If you wind up in a remote area with a weak Internet connection and you had chosen cloud storage as your backup method, you may find yourself pulling your hair out as your upload progress for images and videos changes from minutes to hours before reaching days. With physical storage – either a flash drive or an external hard drive – you have uninterrupted access and are only charged a one-time purchase fee. The cost and physical size of external hard drives continue to decrease while the storage size increases. Since they are smaller than ever, you can buy an external hard drive that is nearly the same size as a smartphone. Of course, this means you will be in charge of protecting the device and constantly backing up files yourself, but you also don't need an Internet connection to do so or to access the files. It's a small price to pay to ensure you don't lose your digital memories.

Of course, accidents happen. Just one spill of water, beer, or a minty mojito and your electronics might be ruined. Luckily, there are well-made, durable cases for just about any device. If you have a camera, get a case. If you're bringing a smartphone, get a case. If you purchased an external hard drive, get a case. See the pattern? Most electronics are made of plastic or lightweight metal and crush pretty easily. Keep in mind, too, that you are under pressure to pack many things in a small space, and one instance of mishandling your bag can damage your devices.

 This brand seems legit. What's the worst that could happen?

Before leaving the United States, we decided to purchase a Kodak Zx3, which is a hand-sized HD waterproof video camera. It was inexpensive (around $100 USD) and a model that Mike was already familiar using. The camera could screw into a tripod, go underwater, and was designed to survive rough handling. We happily used it for nine months until, while snorkeling, saltwater flooded the camera through the battery door and fried it. For a solid month, we worked with Kodak to try to get a replacement. They were willing to replace it since the incident happened with the first year of purchase, and therefore within its warranty. However, they needed us to mail it back to the United States before they could ship us a new one. It didn't seem like a problem, but the caveat was that they would only mail the replacement to a U.S. address. Even if they mailed it to Mike's parents who then sent it overseas, by the time it was all said and done, we would be without a camera for too long and it would cost us quite a bit in international postage and missed video opportunities.

Luckily, we were supposed to meet a friend in Thailand in a few weeks who was traveling from the United States. The tight timeline didn't afford us the chance to get the replacement Kodak camera; however, he offered himself up as an electronics mule. If we found a camera we wanted, he would buy it in the United States and hand it off to us when we saw him. It was a great idea since the purchase could be made from our home country and the device would be covered by the warranty.

After a week or so of research, we decided to get a GoPro Hero3 White. This is a tiny compact camera that adrenaline sports athletes affix to helmets, bike handles, and even surfboards. They come with waterproof housing and are pretty durable, but they are also expensive, at more than triple the cost of what we originally paid for the Kodak. Mike felt this was a worthy expenditure since we had a few months left in our trip, though Tara was more skeptical.

Ultimately, we also had to purchase a mount, an extra battery, and more memory cards since the GoPro takes a microSD card while our other camera used SD cards. All of these items arrived just in time for Songkran, which is New Year's Day in Thailand and celebrated with an incredible water festival. The camera took great footage and the case protected it from getting wet. Then, two weeks later, we were in Myanmar recording the Golden Rock, a Buddhist pilgrimage site, when the GoPro fried two of our memory cards (it fried one, so we tried to use another not knowing what had happened, then it fried the second card). We would have still been upset if it broke in Thailand, but in Myanmar our options were even more limited for repairing and replacing the camera. GoPro ultimately agreed to ship a new camera, but under the condition that we mail them the defective camera first, paying for shipping ourselves.

Needless to say, in addition to costing more time and money than we first expected, this was a hassle we would have rather avoided. Sometimes the most recognizable brand is not necessarily the best one. Tara tries not to say "I told you so" whenever this story come up, but Mike doesn't really blame her for doing it.

In the event that damage does occur, you may be able to fix the problem yourself. Pack a small electronics first aid kit with a lens cleaner, tiny screwdriver, cotton swabs, duct tape, and a tiny can of air. Even if you aren't technologically savvy, these items can help you solve a considerable number of problems. Worst-case scenario: if basic self-troubleshooting doesn't help your situation, try to find an authorized retailer to repair or replace your device. However, odds are that getting something repaired or replaced without additional fees on your end, even if it's within warranty, are slim to none. Most warranties (including the additional care that you likely paid extra for) cover repairs only in the country of purchase. Keep this in mind when buying electronics while on the road. It may seem like a deal to buy a DSLR for less than in your home country, but you might also be out of luck if something unfortunate happens to it.

Now that you've completed this chapter and have a sense of the electronics and features you want to be on the lookout for, it's time to narrow your device choices to up to four different models or brands. Then you should compare the feedback on the companies themselves. If a manufacturer does not seem to stand by their products, avoid them. Next, read reviews for specific models to identify the pros and cons. This approach will help you narrow your choices to one or two finalists. After you do this research, go to a store to check out the devices in person (especially if you plan to buy them online). You'll want to make sure you are comfortable with their actual size and weight. By this point, you should have a good feeling of what you want to buy – so go for it!

Purchasing electronics isn't the last step, though. Prior to leaving, give yourself plenty of time to play with your electronics, test them, and, if need be, return or exchange them. You want to make sure you feel comfortable using them and all their functions. After all, these are expensive decisions, so don't feel pressured to keep something that doesn't quite meet your expectations.

CHAPTER IN REVIEW

❑   Shoot for the stars, then ratchet in your expectations. Make an electronics wish list, and then remove items until you're left with what makes the most sense for your trip.

❑   Electronics can be heavy, bulky, and expensive. Try to minimize what you bring by buying multipurpose devices.

❑   Shop wisely. Do not overspend on electronics that have features and capabilities you will never use.

❑   Bring an inexpensive global phone, if only for emergency use. We recommend using one that will accept a SIM card from any country around the world.

❑   A camera is a must-bring item. Do your research and compare features so you buy the type and level of camera that is best for you and your trip.

❑   Electronics and their components can be prone to failure in certain conditions, so invest in cases to protect them from the elements.

❑   Batteries and external battery packs are worthy investments for power-hungry devices.

❑   Protect your data online with a virtual private network and physically with an external hard drive.

❑   Buy the most expensive electronics on your list months before your departure date so you can use them and get comfortable with their settings and, if necessary, return or exchange them.

CHAPTER 10

Wrapping Up the Larger Things in Life
3 Months to 1 Month Prior to Departure

YOU'RE IN THE home stretch — just one month out — and are probably so excited that you want to scream about your trip from the top of buildings. But don't scream too loud just yet. It's likely that you've kept more than just a few people in the dark about your big plans. While this is exciting news for you, it will probably shock others, and their reaction may surprise you. Your loved ones may have mixed feelings about your quitting your job to travel around the world. You have to remember that while you have spent the last several months convinced (or still convincing yourself) that you're making the right choice, there are people in your life who have no idea about your plans.

It's important to carefully select those whom you will tell about your trip — and when. That last part is the most important for a couple reasons. First, you wouldn't want to announce it on Facebook or tell coworkers until you have handed in your resignation. Besides being unprofessional, announcing your trip in this way could burn a bridge that you may need when you return. Second, there are undoubtedly some people in your life who you may think won't support the idea in general. Keeping these individuals in the dark until closer to departure will prevent you from carrying their negativity throughout the planning process. You can't know for sure who will be supportive and who will be resentful, so use your best judgment. We'll give you some pointers for telling coworkers, family, and friends.

Announcing your trip at work

After a year of holding your cards close to your chest, it is time to start telling people. Think of this as a controlled release, not a bursting balloon. A controlled release means not posting a status update on your social media accounts that publicize your trip – at least not just yet. By telling too many people too soon, this news will spread beyond your control before you tell key people. If you've been careful, only your family and close friends know about your trip, and now it's time to tell your boss. There are a few things to consider before handing in your resignation letter at work.

It's important that you cleverly manage the information to ensure that your immediate supervisor is the first person in the office to find out about your resignation and the trip. It is disrespectful and unprofessional for him or her to hear about it from others instead of from you directly. Once the two of you discuss it, ask your supervisor how and when to tell coworkers. Being courteous, understanding, and as helpful as possible during this time will allow you to leave on a positive note. This applies to jobs that you may have no intention of returning to later. Leaving your position on good terms will earn you positive references that you'll need in the future, and your employer may even consider you for consulting work or fulltime employment upon your return. Even if you are looking at this trip as a permanent break from your career, you never know when you'll need to use a professional reference, and acting in an unprofessional manner on your way out of the country could ruin that opportunity for you.

 What about a leave of absence?

Depending on the type of position you hold and the relationship you have with your employer, you may be able to negotiate a leave of absence for your trip. Those of you who work for an institution of higher learning have an even better option: you may be able to take a sabbatical. Sabbaticals are usually reserved for professors who have worked at a university for at least seven years, at which point they can take time off to study and travel. It is even better than a leave of absence because it is paid leave.

Although I was not a professor, I had worked in the same department at a university for seven years, and I was hopeful I'd be able to take a sabbatical of sorts. I gave my boss four months' notice, and for months he worked with human resources to try to grant a leave of absence. The only problem ended up being the timing. I had just been promoted a few months earlier to a position that the department created for me. I'll save you the long, drawn-out version and tell you that it was too difficult to make a convincing argument that a position that had just been created could be vacated for more than a year. Ultimately, I worked until the week prior to our departure without reprisal from my employer, and my position was filled soon after I left.

Every situation is unique, and if you can swing a leave of absence or sabbatical, it might be worth approaching your manager sooner than a month before departure to talk it out. However, if you have not been with the same company for several years and feel that you're a valuable asset to the business, it is probably in your best interest to wait until closer to your departure date to inform your employer.

Part of leaving on good terms also includes giving appropriate notice for your resignation. Will you give the customary two weeks' notice, or do you think you need additional time to train coworkers? The most significant problem with giving more than two weeks' notice is that your employer could terminate you immediately or before your anticipated resignation date. You certainly don't want to lose out on a few more paychecks. More than the loss of your income, you may also be relying on your employer-sponsored healthcare to cover travel vaccinations. Getting let go prematurely could jeopardize your benefits coverage, so aside from handling your departure professionally, you should also do so in a way that protects you and your interests.

Knowing which benefits you'll be losing access to and when they terminate should be part of your resignation strategy, which you should formulate a few months prior to leaving. If your job awards hefty quarterly or annual bonuses, you'll want to set your departure date accordingly to ensure you receive these. Additionally, plan to squeeze in one last dental cleaning and physical examination so you can leave knowing the state of your health. Some companies insure their employees through the end of the month in which they quit, while others may end coverage on your last day of employment. It's worth carefully exploring this with your company's human resources division to get the full story. In the United States, there are options to extend your company's health insurance after you leave (through COBRA), but you would be required to pay out of pocket for it. This option can be expensive, but it may be better for you than to go without insurance.

In addition to losing your employer-sponsored benefits, think about the professional information you will lose access to as well. For example, many companies store work history information in their internal database, like your salary history, position description, dates you were hired or promoted, and annual reviews. If you have worked for the same company for several years, you may not be keeping track of all the qualitative reviews and awards you've received as well as successful projects you worked on. It's easy to forget all of the associated details between the time you quit and when you're interviewing again, so having that hard data to pitch to future employers will be valuable.

You may also want to jot down names, email addresses, and telephone numbers of colleagues whom you intend to use as references in the future. Find these people on professional networks like LinkedIn so you can stay connected in the meantime, and ask if they'll submit a public reference for you while your achievements and work ethic are fresh in their mind. Before you connect with them, make sure that your professional profile is fully updated.

As you update your public professional profile, don't forget to work on your personal résumé as well (on your computer and any employment websites you may be a member of). Again, the details of what you've accomplished in your current role may become blurry later if you don't keep track of them now. Pretend that you're going to apply to a new job and update your résumé and cover letter with all applicable information. Then when you return home and are looking for employment, the only work you'll have to do is personalize your documents to each employer and job description. Doing this now will save you a lot of time and stress after your trip ends.

Telling the world about your plans

Remember that burning urge to scream about your incredible trip from the nearest skyscraper? Well, the time has arrived! After you tell your closest family members, friends, and those at your workplace, the next step is to tell anyone willing to listen. Okay, maybe don't stop strangers on the street, but at least you can now clue in everyone else, including announcing it on social media. With the veil of secrecy gone, telling everyone in your life will have a threefold benefit: you will likely receive unsolicited advice for destinations you might visit, you might get offers to introduce you to friends living abroad, and you might even find out that some people you know are now living abroad and might offer to help or host you. These are priceless offers that should not be turned down, no matter how knowledgeable and travel-savvy you think you are.

 ## The benefits of a local's perspective

While traveling up the coast of Croatia, our last stop in the country was the small port city of Rijeka. Guidebooks brushed it off as a drab transit point for those traveling overland between Croatia and Italy. Based on what we read, we expected to spend a day there before feeling compelled to move on. However, we ended up interacting with a Croatian from Rijeka who had nothing but great things to say about her city. Before we knew it, we had a packed itinerary that required a couple days to complete. Going with our gut, we booked a few nights, and it turned out to be a great decision.

The local's suggestions filled our days with unique experiences, like eating lunch at a restaurant that serves freshly caught fish and closes once they run out and climbing a high hill to an outlook that offers a beautiful panorama of the Adriatic Sea and the surrounding rolling hills. When we finally left, we wondered if the guidebook writers had even spent time in the same city that we just had. If we had only gone off the reviews and online recommendations, we would have skipped a wonderful gem.

Even though you'll receive a lot of support and admiration for your trip, you should still expect a wide array of reactions. Those who don't share your mindset may be perplexed, disinterested, or dismissive. "You're lucky; did you win the lottery?" and "It must be nice to be able to do something like that" are two common responses we received from acquaintances and some coworkers. When you hear comments like this, remember the sacrifices you're making and how hard you worked over the past year to reorganize your commitments and your life in order to make this dream a reality. Don't let other people's jealousy or lack of empathy ruin your fun. Just like everyone else, you do have obligations, but you also have a passion and the self-control to realize your goals. Tell them, "I'm not lucky. I'm just proactive."

Considering the amount of time and effort you have expended for the past year to make this journey a reality – and your willingness to quit your job and travel for a significant period – you would think that your commitment to this goal is apparent. However, the idea of taking a trip like this does not appeal to everyone, and some people will speak without thinking. At one of our big "coming out" parties, one acquaintance flat-out said, "Traveling like that sounds fun, for about a week." Remember, it's not your job to convince others that this is something they should do. You should continue to focus on the positive aspects and how this trip is right for you.

Having a positive attitude is infectious, and the overwhelming majority of people we told about our big trip were thrilled to follow our upcoming adventure. One friend offered her home as a temporary mailing address, "When you see souvenirs or anything on the road that you want to buy but can't carry with you, send it to me. I'll hold onto it for you until you get home." Others offered up a closet or an attic to store our remaining belongings. The outpouring of generous support was touching and, in many cases, extremely helpful.

Wrapping up life at home

In addition to publicly announcing your trip, you still have very important action items left to complete in your last month at home. This is your chance to finalize plans and remaining paperwork before you hit the road. You should be close to or completely debt-free (or have a foolproof plan for taking care of your remaining debt) and your car, home, and any possessions you're not keeping should be ready to be sold, donated, or thrown away. If you are living in an apartment, you should prepare your move-out notice in advance (most management companies require 30 days' notice).

It is also time to start cutting the cord to your financial responsibilities. Think about the monthly bills you pay now that will need to terminate when you leave, and make sure you have a plan for how and when to end them (like contacting your Internet provider to cancel your service). If you haven't yet finished the time requirement for a specific contract – for example, a two-year cell phone contract – crunch the numbers to determine whether early termination fees will be more or less expensive than paying out the remainder of your contract. If fulfilling your contractual obligations is less expensive, then obviously go that route, but ensure you don't overpay. In some cases, yearlong contracts won't automatically terminate when the contractual period ends; they instead switch to a month-to-month commitment and continue to bill you until you take the required steps to terminate the service. Nip this in the bud for all services and subscriptions you won't need on the road by canceling your contracts before or as they expire.

It's nearly unavoidable to have financial obligations you cannot escape, such as loan repayments (such as credit cards, student loans, or a mortgage) and services you cannot suspend or terminate (like healthcare, car insurance, and a storage unit). The best course of action for paying these monthly bills while on the road is to set up and activate automatic bill pay. This is a hassle-free option since you shouldn't need to take further action after activation. Just be sure that the withdrawals are coming from a bank account that contains enough money to support the bills starting now and lasting through your trip. You'll want to start doing this at least one billing cycle before your departure to work out any issues you might encounter.

You'll also need to set up travel notifications for any debit and credit cards you'll carry during your trip. Completing this task will undoubtedly save you from unnecessary stress on the road (like being declined at the register because your purchase set off a fraud alert). This can be done easily by calling customer service or logging into your online account. All you have to do is specify which countries you will be traveling in during the upcoming months, then continue to do this every few months during your trip or if you add a new country to your itinerary. That's it! Once the card company knows where you'll be, they won't flag or block your account for suspicious activity when you use your card in the specified countries (you should still check your statements regularly for fraudulent activity when you have a secure Internet connection).

Keeping your bank and credit card companies privy to your travel plans is crucial to protecting your information. You should also go one step further and temporarily freeze your credit accounts to protect your identity. In the United States, there are three credit bureaus (Experian, Equifax, and TransUnion) that monitor your credit history and maintain your credit score. The freeze will prevent other people (and yourself, for that matter) from opening a new line of credit in your name, which you most likely won't need to do anyway while traveling around the world. This can include loans, credit cards, and telephone lines. The minimal time it takes to request the freeze is worth it for the level of protection it offers. Each credit bureau has its own rules for how to complete this process, and you might be charged a small fee depending on the bureau and where you live. When the process is complete, they will send you a confirmation letter and sometimes a PIN. Be sure to keep these documents in a safe place, as the information will be necessary to lift the freeze. After you return home, you can remove the temporary freeze as easily as you placed it. Again, you may encounter a nominal fee depending on the location of your permanent address.

If you're an American citizen, another protection you should consider is the Smart Traveler Enrollment Program (STEP), a free service provided by the State Department. When enrolling in this program, you select the countries you will be visiting and STEP sends your information to the local U.S. embassies so they can contact you if there's a national emergency, civil unrest, or if your friends or family need to get in touch with you in an emergency. STEP will also email you information that alerts you to safety issues or travel warnings in the countries you specified. Enrolling in this program is just an additional step to help ensure you're safe and informed while traveling abroad.

Planning for the absolute worst-case scenario

When planning extended travel, it is important to prepare for all possible scenarios, and especially for the worst-case scenario. This isn't a welcome thought, but by "worst" we mean death. Just as the risk is real at home, it's also real when you travel. When you purchased travel insurance, you likely noticed that most policies come with clauses for death, dismemberment, and reclamation of your physical remains (or your travel partner's). This coverage should help navigate the difficulties (both logistically and financially) of an accident while you are abroad. However, insurance does not automatically create beneficiaries, nor should it be considered a will or living trust. If you do not proactively create the necessary legal documents to designate beneficiaries for your assets and possessions, they will be divvied up arbitrarily by the state, which usually takes a hefty cut from the process. Setting up the necessary legal documents before you step foot outside of your native country will should prevent such a nightmare in that unlikely worst-case scenario.

 Finding a lawyer

Our trip, though bound to be an exciting adventure, caused us to think about the bigger, scarier picture too. Neither of us had any legal documents in place at the time, so we knew we needed a lawyer to create a will, living will, and power of attorney. My employer had a legal retainer program that resembled dental or medical insurance in concept. You paid a small fee each pay period for access to legal counsel that was provided either free or at a heavily discounted rate. This was a perfect option for us since preparing these legal documents for our trip was the only reason we needed a lawyer.

The caveat to receiving this coverage was that I had to sign up for it during open enrollment, which falls in November. Luckily, we already knew we needed a lawyer to draft these documents (we weren't leaving until the following June but had been planning our trip for months by the time open enrollment began), so I signed up for the program. We waited until about two months prior to departure to find an attorney, and he took care of all the documents we needed in one afternoon. Because these documents fell under the plan's coverage, we did not have to pay anything out of pocket for the lawyer's services. We did need to have them notarized to make them official, which cost a small fee, but that was it.

If your employer does not offer such a program or you've passed the open enrollment period, another way to save money on this service is to look for law schools that offer pro bono document preparation.

Begin by preparing a will and living trust with a legal professional. Both of these contain inheritance instructions but are used in different ways. Think of a will as the final say on what will happen to assets that are in your name when you pass away, such as finances, property, and material objects. You'll be responsible for assigning beneficiaries to these items so they can be distributed to your liking. The document will also specify any last wishes and funeral arrangements as well as assign legal guardianship for any children you may have who are still under the age of 18. Without a last will, a probate court will be in charge of deciding how to divide your assets, taking with it a healthy cut for the state and tying up your finances in the process.

A living trust, on the other hand, typically wouldn't go through probate because you will transfer your property to the trust while you're still alive and well. We don't want to go into too many details here because these are very technical documents that need to be discussed with a lawyer. If you haven't already created a will and living trust, you should contact a legal professional to determine which is right for you.

Next, you'll want to create a living will. This is an important document to have drawn up, regardless of your travel plans. A living will details your medical treatment preferences if you're in a state in which you are no longer able to express your desires or give informed consent. If you fall into a coma, are put on life support, or are considered to be in a vegetative mental state and cannot speak for yourself, your living will dictates your treatment and overrides the desires or beliefs that your family may have.

Whatever intentions or personal beliefs you have when it comes to end-of-life issues are yours, and this document ensures that no one else chooses for you.

Power of attorney (POA) is another important legal document that grants a secondary party the ability to sign official papers and speak on your behalf. The benefits to assigning a POA during extended travel abroad are numerous. This person can sign and file your tax documents for you, call your credit card company to dispute a charge, and write a check or withdraw funds from your bank account. As you can see, granting someone power of attorney is no small matter. This person has absolute binding power to act in your name until you revoke the POA, so you need to make sure this responsibility goes to someone you trust completely. Without designating a POA, no one can represent you in your absence; even your parents do not have the legal authority.

 ## We grant you the power to legally represent us

Our decision to make Mike's mother our POA was a difficult one. We did not want to hurt anyone's feelings, as all of our parents are responsible and trustworthy. However, it boiled down to us wanting to be as minimal a burden as possible. Tara's parents were planning to do a lot of travel during our trip, so we worried that if time-sensitive documents were sent to their address, it might be an inconvenience to them. For Mike's mother to act as our POA, she had to be willing to be on call and take the time to do things and follow up on our behalf.

We hoped we wouldn't need to bother her for anything but our taxes, but Mike had an issue that required enacting the POA almost immediately after we started our trip. Prior to leaving, Mike was trying to get a refund from his health insurance for overpaying for travel vaccinations. He spent hours calling doctors and the insurance company and faxing, emailing, and mailing in proof of his claim. The process was a hassle and quite time-consuming, but Mike wasn't able to resolve the issue before our trip began. It therefore translated into a months-long time commit for our POA, which thankfully resulted in obtaining the refund he was owed.

This story illustrates how important it is to choose an individual who is responsible and willing and able to find the time to fight on your behalf in addition to signing documents for you.

When you do draft the power of attorney, have your lawyer create two original documents. You'll want to keep one in a safe place and give the other to the person who will act on your behalf. But this is just the first step. In order for them to have access to your accounts, they will need to submit notarized copies to any institution you want them to have access to. This may take some time, so it is best to call each company to see what their process is so you can complete this step prior to leaving. You wouldn't want to be on the road and have an issue sit in limbo because they didn't have a copy of the POA document on file.

Not all of your documents will need to be prepared by a lawyer. Beneficiary information can be completed without one. This applies to financial accounts like a certificate of deposit (CD), stock market shares, savings accounts, and if you contribute to a 401(k), IRA, annuity account, or life insurance policy. For each of these accounts, review the beneficiary form prior to leaving for your trip to ensure that all information is updated. Completing this form allows the financial institutions to transfer your assets to a person or multiple people you designate, even if you do not yet have a will. That is done through transfer on death (TOD) and payable on death (POD) instructions. A TOD form is used by brokerage or investment accounts, while banks use PODs. Be sure to make a record of all your open accounts and leave that information with your power of attorney.

Keeping your documents safe

After you finalize all the documents we just discussed, consult with your lawyer to see whether he or she would be willing to retain copies of the documents free of charge or for a small fee. If not, make sure you protect them along with other important documents you have – for example, your travel partner's and your birth certificates, social security cards, marriage license, previous years' tax filings, stock holdings, and bank and retirement account information. You can likely think of other sensitive documents that you will need to protect and store securely as well.

Gather all of this paperwork into a folder and lock it in a safe deposit box at a bank or in a family member's or trusted friend's in-home, fireproof safe. Just be sure that the documents are accessible to your appointed POA.

Next, you need to think about all the important documents you will be traveling with, such as a passport, credit cards, and a driver's license. Print a couple color copies of each and scan them as well to create digital files. Keep one paper copy hidden within your carry-on luggage (separate from the originals) and give the other to your travel partner. Put the digital files onto two encrypted flash drives and give one to your power of attorney and bring the other with you on your trip. Also create a password-protected text file for each flash drive with your bank account and credit card numbers, account login information (username, password, PIN, security questions, and mother's maiden name), and their respective customer service phone numbers (most financial institutions offer a toll-free number for domestic calls and an international direct number, which is a collect call, when traveling abroad). Hopefully these documents will not be necessary during your trip, but at least they will be easily accessible should you or your POA need them.

Your new permanent address

Since you're giving up your home while you travel, you will need to establish a permanent address for mail forwarding and tax purposes. The easiest and best option is to use the home address of the person serving as your POA. This person has the legal right to open your mail and respond to messages, like a jury summons, and let them know you are traveling.

If you do not want your power of attorney's address associated with your contact information, you could always look into registering with a mailbox service near where your POA lives. A mailbox service differs from a post office box in the sense that they operate out of a verifiable physical address through a company (such as United Parcel Service, or UPS) for a fee. Choosing to use your power of attorney's address or a mailbox service instead of a post office box will fulfill one of the requirements of United States citizens: maintaining a domicile in the United States. Unless you plan to renounce your citizenship, it is good to know that a P.O. Box is not considered a domicile; the other two are, so they qualify as proof of residency in most states (which should allow you to register for a driver's license, among other benefits). However, it is always best to research each state's requirements.

After you establish a permanent address, take preemptive measures whenever you can so that necessary parties are aware of your trip before you go. This includes updating your address information with any company that has it on file, including loan and financial institutions, credit card companies, medical professionals, insurance companies, your local Board of Elections, any company that might send you a bill, and of course your family and friends. The most important entity to file your change of address with is the United States Postal Service (USPS). Submitting your new address to USPS is the best way to ensure that mail is forwarded to the right location while you are traveling (they will do this free of charge for up to one year). Keep any confirmation letters that USPS sends you for your change of address, because you may need the reference code to make future adjustments. It is also important to have the person who is collecting your forwarded mail inform the original sender of your new address. Again, this is easiest accomplished if this is done through your POA since they have the legal right to request this adjustment.

Say farewell to some of the people and things you love, for now

Travel is exciting and gaining new experiences is an important aspect of it, but the familiarity and comfort of your home, city, and different locations that have special meaning to you will soon be a memory. Your trip will obviously keep you from some of your favorite things, so this is your last chance to soak in as much as you possibly can before you leave. Think about the simple pleasures of enjoying a home-cooked meal, sleeping in your own bed, soaking in a bathtub, and showering without wearing plastic flip-flops. Don't forget to appreciate what your city offers, like going to your favorite restaurant where the staff knows your order, enjoying a newly released movie in the theater without subtitles or dubbing, and visiting your favorite park, trail, or scenic spot. In your hurry to finalize everything before you leave, you may not have stopped to think about how much you may miss simple and familiar pleasures. Definitely take some time to appreciate all the things inside your comfort zone.

Before you get down to the final weeks and days prior to departure, you need to plan one more thing – your farewell party! Friends and family may tell you now that they want to meet up with you on the road, but there is no guarantee, and it's actually quite difficult to plan and pull off while you're traveling. Instead, gather everyone up to celebrate this new chapter in your life and send you off with a proper farewell. Plus, it's a great way to spend time with those who you may not have seen often during your trip preparation.

Your going away party can be as low-key or as much of a blowout as you want it to be. Have it in your empty home, in a bar, outside at a state park, or at a location that's meaningful to you. Besides seeing everyone one last time before your trip, this is a great opportunity to collect their updated contact information so you can send them postcards from the road. People get so few desirable pieces of snail mail these days that they are bound to smile when your postcard arrives from Egypt or India or Argentina. It's a great way to loosely stay in touch and let them know you're thinking of them.

Likewise, make sure you have everyone's email address or Skype username so you have another way to stay in touch and connect while abroad.

You should also give friends and family a way to track your whereabouts by creating and maintaining a blog or even a map online with your tentative route. This will not only let them know where you plan to go, it may also help you synchronize a rendezvous or two.

There are many benefits to maintaining a blog while traveling, and we encourage you to do so. First, it's a great way to keep your loved ones informed of where you are and what you're doing without sending mass or individual emails. Also, it's a simple way to help you remember what you did, when, and where. If you include images and videos, it becomes a combination journal-photo album-documentary for you to look back at right after your trip and years down the road.

If you don't want to create a public blog, you could turn on privacy settings so that only those with a password can access the site or you can consider writing in a paper journal. We strongly encourage you to keep some kind of account of what you did during your trip. Even with timestamps, your memories of pictures and videos may blur, so by keeping a detailed account of your journey, you'll be able to transport yourself back to when and where you may have been for a thrilling experience. With the right angle and a good sales pitch, you might even be able to turn your journal into a book.

Everything must go

At the beginning of this book, we talked about the importance of starting early, from saving money to reducing your possessions to other aspects of pre-departure planning. Hopefully you have been able to get rid of underused and unwanted physical possessions. If you still have items to get rid of, consider donating them or hosting a fire sale where everything must go. Even if you only make a couple bucks off some items, it's better than hauling them to the trash or receiving no money at all for things of value. Take this opportunity to cut the clutter so you can return from your trip with a clean slate.

In the end, it's likely that you will have a few unwanted items left over (things like spices, liquor, and cleaning supplies). Consider donating these to charity or give them to friends, family, or your neighbors. Afterward, you'll need to box up and store your remaining possessions according to how you planned, whether that means bringing them to a storage unit or to a friend or family member's home.

Now that you're within sight of your departure date, you need to make these final hard decisions. Besides time, they're the only things standing in your way of your incredible trip!

CHAPTER IN REVIEW

❑ Make sure your supervisor is the first person in your office to know about your resignation and trip.

❑ Update your résumé, cover letter, and online professional profile while your achievements are still fresh in your mind.

❑ Place a temporary freeze on your credit through Experian, Equifax, and TransUnion to help protect yourself.

❑ Assign beneficiaries to all your financial accounts and create a will, living trust, and living will with a lawyer.

❑ Ask the most trustworthy person in your life if he or she will act as your power of attorney while you're traveling. With a lawyer, create the necessary legal document to make it official.

❑ Submit proof of power of attorney to any institution you may need your POA to contact on your behalf.

❑ Make physical and digital back-up copies of every important document you have. Split up hard copies between you and your travel partner. Create a password-protected text file with your bank account and credit card numbers, account login information, and their respective customer service phone numbers. Put all digital documents on two encrypted flash drives – one for yourself and one for your power of attorney.

❑ Inform all pertinent financial institutions of your international travel plans.

❑ Determine where your mailing address will be while you travel and register it with any companies that have your address on file or send you mail, as well as with the postal service.

❑ Throw an awesome farewell party! Gather contact information from your friends and family so you can send them postcards during your travels.

❑ Start a blog so others can follow your journey and so you can look back at it one day and reminisce.

❑ Hold a fire sale so you can sell any final possessions that you aren't going to take with you. Donate any that are left over to charity or give them to friends, family, or neighbors.

❑ Pack up the things you want to save and bring them to wherever you plan to store them while you're gone.

CHAPTER 11

Managing Your Trip Budget
1 Month Prior to Departure

BY NOW, YOU and your travel partner have (hopefully!) become great teammates while you prepare for your life-changing adventure. However, working together as a cohesive unit on the road isn't always easy – you're only human and bound to have disagreements – but by optimizing each other's strengths, you'll help reduce the number of potential tiffs. Do this by giving each other jobs to be specifically accountable for. For example, if you have a knack for finding the best hotels, then you should be in charge of booking accommodations during your trip. But if you yourself are prone to losing small items, give your travel partner the permanent job of keeping track of the hotel room key. That way you'll always know who is grabbing it before you leave the room and who has it when you return after a day of sightseeing. This will help eliminate instances of thinking that the other person took the key and getting locked out.

Similarly, if you've been managing most of the finances so far, continue that role on the road too. Leaving for your trip shouldn't put an end to the good habits you developed during pre-departure planning. Since you probably won't have a steady income on the road, keeping track of your spending habits will be even more important than it was during the months leading up to your departure. After all, you don't want to end your trip early because you're running out of money.

By this point, you should know the total amount you can spend during your trip, which should be the balance in your World Travel Fund savings account plus any money left in the account that maintains your current lifestyle (excluding, of course, your No-Touch Account that contains money for loan repayments and your return cushion). We hope you were able to meet or surpass your ultimate savings goal, but if you didn't, you will need to make some adjustments to your proposed itinerary or travel style so you don't spend all your savings before you are ready to return. Adjustments could include cooking for yourselves more often than eating out, Couchsurfing when you can, staying in more low-cost accommodations than you anticipated, replacing a few expensive countries with countries that won't hit your budget as hard, or occasionally volunteering or working for hostels in exchange for free room and board.

After you and your travel partner discuss these necessary adjustments, if they're applicable, you (or whoever has been managing most of the finances) should figure out how you will spend your savings on the road. The best way to guide your spending is to refer back to the calculations you made for the cost of each region on your tentative route. Examine potential costs for food, transportation, accommodations, and entertainment and set a per diem for both you and your travel partner (separately or together – whichever works best for your travel style) based on these estimates. Then, use your best judgment to reduce your per diem a little so you can aim to come in under budget.

The goal in reducing your per diem is to put those additional funds toward emergency situations. An emergency could be an injury, needing to leave a city immediately, paying for a flight because trains are booked solid, or having to opt for an expensive hotel because your hostel lost your reservation. Dip into these funds as you need them, and if you don't end up spending it all, you can use it to extend your trip, spoil yourself toward the end of your trip, or to help support you after your trip.

Tracking your spending abroad

Keeping track of how you spend every penny and dollar may sound excessive, but we highly encourage you to take the time to do this, especially during your first few months of travel. You'll get a feel for how you're spending your money and have the detailed information you need to determine whether your habits will be sustainable through the rest of your trip.

 A standard day for a traveler in Portugal

Let's examine a day in Lisbon, Portugal. Before you arrive in the country, you'll want to create a daily budget. We're going to estimate an €80 per diem for two people. Here's how it breaks down by category:

Sample daily budget for Portugal: €80
- Accommodations budget: €27
- Food budget: €33
- Activities/Miscellaneous budget: €20

Now we'll look at the minor and major expenses you should keep track of while traveling. Consider these actual expenditures for one day in the country:

One day in Lisbon, Portugal: €84
- Two hostel beds in a 12-bed room: €26
- Breakfast (2 pastries and 2 coffees): €6
- 1 liter of water: €1
- Soda: €1
- Tour guide's tip for a free walking tour: €10
- Tram ride (2 tickets): €3
- 1 liter of water: €1
- Lunch (2 Francesinhas sandwiches and 2 sodas): €18
- Tram ride (2 tickets): €3
- Dinner (food from a grocery store): €10
- Bottle of port: €5

This seems like a pretty standard sightseeing day around town, and it might be difficult for you to recognize what changes can be made to stay within budget. Luckily, the tracked expenses from this day are all you need to analyze your spending habits and identify where you could save money in the future.

Let's start at the top of this list where your day essentially begins. It appears that you've paid for accommodations in a hostel that doesn't offer complimentary breakfast. Many hostels, especially in Europe, offer small perks that you can't even find at hotels, like complimentary breakfast and Wi-Fi, and their cost is usually on par with hostels that exclude these benefits. By booking accommodations that include breakfast, you will not only avoid the €6 charge for pastries and coffees, but you could also take a pastry or a slice of bread as a snack for later.

Beverage expenses, excluding water, are great to examine if you want to reduce your spending every week. Some travelers view soda and alcohol as luxury items while on the road, not as necessary daily expenses, because they aren't required for your survival. These nice little things add up and take away money from other possible purchases. Sure, you should treat yourself, but do it every now and then instead of daily. Another way to save on beverages is to buy a reusable bottle to fill with water if you find yourself in a country that has potable tap water. The bottle will be a one-time expense that will ultimately save you money every day. (You could also look into purchasing a LifeStraw so you can drink tap water safely.)

Finally, let's look at transportation. Some distances are just too far to walk if you want to make it to your destination during daylight hours. Sometimes, though, what seems far on a map might actually be an easy and scenic walk. Not only is walking free, it will also help you learn the layout of the city better and give you the opportunity to take a detour if there's something you want to see or photograph.

Once you hit the road, use this method to examine a typical day so you can come up with a few ideas to reduce daily expenses. It may be difficult to stick to your budget perfectly every day, and that's ok. For each day when you overspend, you will likely have a day when you come in under budget. Overall, you just want to keep tabs on what could be considered excessive purchases (which are different from splurging on exciting experiences), just like you've been doing at home while saving for the trip.

After reviewing your daily expenditures for a few months, you'll become a pro at recognizing where to reduce spending or which expenses to cut out altogether. But you have to set yourself up for success, and the only way to do that is with an organized money tracking system.

We recommend keeping track of all expenses in a notebook or on your smartphone each day and as you incur them (there are plenty of budgeting and expense tracking apps out there to help). Notice we say to track them as you make them. If you wait to compile your expenditures until the end of the day, you may forget a few little things, like street food, a postcard, or a tip you gave to a guide. Taking notes allows you to later transfer the information to a spreadsheet that you maintain in the cloud (like a Google document) or on a personal computer (if you brought one). You'll want to do this each day, as your notes will be pages long if you wait to do it weekly or monthly. If the task becomes daunting, you're less likely to complete it.

The word "spreadsheet" might have caught your eye, or maybe you completely ignored it. If you've never created or maintained a spreadsheet before, know that it's not as intimidating as it may look. You don't have to learn complicated formulas or create pivot tables to track your money. There are plenty of free online tutorials for beginners that won't take up much of your time, and we highly recommend taking advantage of them before you leave. Once you've gone through the training, you should start practicing your new skills immediately by keeping track of your spending at home in the same way that you will on the road.

 Reminders to help keep you sane

The more specific you are in your planning, the more accurate your budget will be. If you only know that a country is "expensive," that won't help you estimate how much money to allocate toward your stay there. You should've already researched the average costs associated with each country or region you'll be visiting, but if there are potential destinations that you have not looked into, do the additional research now to give you an idea of what you might spend there. Completing this extra legwork early should prevent you from panicking after you land in a new country.

Similarly, knowing the approximate cost of activities you want to indulge in will help you spend your splurge money more wisely. It may cause you to decide that you'd rather get a massage in Thailand instead of France, go SCUBA diving in Malaysia instead of Australia, or upgrade to a five-star hotel in India rather than South Africa.

Beyond researching costs, remain cognizant of high season, large local festivals, and countrywide holidays, because prices will soar during these times. Even if you're not attending a local festival, you'll have no choice but to pay higher accommodation prices if you're staying in town or nearby since all out-of-towners compete to book the same hotels.

On the topic of accommodations, know that hostels aren't always dingy and resorts aren't always worth the higher price tag. Take the time to research options so you can receive the greatest return from the money you're spending. Even if you are indifferent to where you sleep, you should still research your options instead of just walking around town when you arrive. Think of how much quicker it is to locate nightly rates by searching online versus going door-to-door to get quotes. A very cursory search will reveal which accommodations in a given city have solid ratings from reviewers and are well appointed for their cost. Doing a few minutes of research may result in a better night's sleep, a complimentary breakfast, and even keep you out of the bad part of town (or an area that's far away from everything you want to see and do).

If as you track your purchases you notice that you're spending more than you budgeted and cannot find where to cut (or don't want to), think about why that is. You may find that you can't stay on budget because you incorrectly predicted your travel style or that it's changed over time. The type of travelers we were at the beginning of our trip barely matched the travelers we became by the end. Just redo your math to match your current travel style. Set aside time to calculate a new budget that you can match or beat without running out of money on the road or using money from your return fund. As you're recalculating, you may realize that you need to reevaluate your itinerary or how long you plan to travel. There is also a way around that. Don't forget the many options that travelers have available to them to save money, such as staying with locals for free (through a community like Couchsurfing), picking up odd jobs to create a small income, and volunteering or working in exchange for room and board. Adding these experiences to your trip could help you get back on track over time.

If you do utilize these options, approach each experience in a positive way. Volunteer work will ultimately become part of your trip, and it might even be one of the most memorable things you do (it could also be résumé-worthy). Keep an open mind and remember that every experience during this time will be unique to your trip, and that in itself is unforgettable.

CHAPTER IN REVIEW

❑ Designate a trip CFO (chief financial officer) who will track expenses as they occur and keep the two of you on budget.

❑ Create a per diem for both you and your travel partner, but then try to reduce it slightly. If you hit this lower goal, you'll be able to save money for emergencies.

❑ Write down expenses as you make them and transfer your notes into a spreadsheet at the end of each day so they don't pile up and become too overwhelming of a task to complete.

❑ Review your spending habits on a regular basis for at least a few months to identify superfluous purchases and ways you can cut back.

❑ If you've maximized your money and are still spending more than you budgeted, reevaluate your itinerary or the length of time you're traveling so you don't run out of money during your trip. To help, you can look into working or volunteering in exchange for room and board.

❑ Consider freelancing or picking up a short-term local job to earn money quickly as long as it won't negatively impact your trip.

Congratulations! You have created your escape and are now ready to take your trip!

We hope that the recommendations in this handbook will help you reach your ultimate happiness. If you found *Create Your Escape* to be helpful, please take a moment to let fellow travelers know by leaving a review on your favorite retailer's site.

If you haven't already downloaded the free checklists and worksheets that supplement this book, go to http://twotravelaholics.com/create-your-escape and type in the password TRAVELNOW to download the files.

We enjoy connecting with fellow travelers, so if you have any questions, you can email us at info@twotravelaholics.com.

Good luck with your preparation, and safe travels!

-Mike and Tara Shubbuck

ACKNOWLEDGEMENTS

We want to thank our loving parents, René and Randy Arrowsmith and Karen and Tom Shubbuck, who nurtured an ever-growing wanderlust since our early days. Family trips and weekend vacations from childhood gave rise to a desire to see more of our country as well as the countries beyond our borders.

We are forever grateful to Lisa and Rick Arrowsmith, who picked us up from Dulles airport at the end of our RTW trip on July 31, 2013, and told us we had a home to stay in until we were ready to leave. Without their continuous support, this book may have never gotten off the ground.

To Nancy Jones, our editor, thank you for the selfless hours you put in to edit our final manuscript. Amanda Stefano's enthusiasm and creativity has thankfully been with us for years, helping us through a Two Travelaholics logo redesign and the gorgeous cover of *Create Your Escape*, our first book.

Our early editors Kiara Kerwin, Susie Monahan, and Shirley Blanchard gave us feedback on our first drafts and helped ensure our vision was well-crafted and moving in the right direction.

Thank you to our family and those who have accepted us as members of their own. All of you who believed in us and supported our wild dreams in various ways over the years are part of the momentum that continues to push us toward more great adventures.

ABOUT THE AUTHORS

MIKE AND TARA SHUBBUCK quit their jobs and sold almost all of their possessions in 2012 to travel around the world for 14 months on an extended honeymoon. Branding themselves in the online travel community as Two Travelaholics, they are known for their conversations with fellow wanderlusters about travel, food, concerts, and craft beer. Mike and Tara live in Washington, D.C.

Connect with Mike and Tara:

 twitter.com/2travelaholics

 facebook.com/TwoTravelaholics

 youtube.com/shubbuck

Discover more by Mike and Tara:

 http://TwoTravelaholics.com

15994229R00159

Printed in Great Britain
by Amazon